LET'S (NOT)
TALK ABOUT
(TRANSGENDER) SEX

ALSO AVAILABLE FROM BLOOMSBURY

What Gender Should Be, Matthew J. Cull
Non-Binary Life, Marquis Bey
Transgender Theory: An Introduction, Ciara Cremin and Abraham Weil

LET'S (NOT) TALK ABOUT (TRANSGENDER) SEX

The Erotic Erasure of Trans Desire & Sexuality

RIKI WILCHINS

BLOOMSBURY ACADEMIC

LONDON • NEW YORK • OXFORD • NEW DELHI • SYDNEY

BLOOMSBURY ACADEMIC

Bloomsbury Publishing Plc, 50 Bedford Square, London, WC1B 3DP, UK
Bloomsbury Publishing Inc, 1359 Broadway, New York, NY 10018, USA
Bloomsbury Publishing Ireland, 29 Earlsfort Terrace, Dublin 2, D02 AY28, Ireland

BLOOMSBURY, BLOOMSBURY ACADEMIC and the Diana logo are trademarks
of Bloomsbury Publishing Plc

First published in Great Britain 2026

Cover design: Charlotte Willow Retief
Cover image © studioretief.com

Bloomsbury Publishing Plc does not have any control over, or responsibility for,
any third-party websites referred to or in this book. All internet addresses given
in this book were correct at the time of going to press. The author and publisher
regret any inconvenience caused if addresses have changed or sites have ceased
to exist, but can accept no responsibility for any such changes.

A catalogue record for this book is available from the British Library.

A catalog record for this book is available from the Library of Congress.

ISBN: HB: 978-1-3505-7451-9
       PB: 978-1-3505-7450-2
       ePDF: 978-1-3505-7452-6
       eBook: 978-1-3505-7453-3

Typeset by Deanta Global Publishing Services, Chennai, India
Printed and bound in Great Britain

For product safety related questions contact productsafety@bloomsbury.com.

To find out more about our authors and books visit www.bloomsbury.com and
sign up for our newsletters.

To Gina and Dylan:
You are my life

CONTENTS

FOREWORD

This book is specifically about what I see the trans studies' general lack of engagement with issues of trans sexuality and embodiment, so I should clarify that I'm talking about the broad thrust of the field as I have come to know it through Anglophone books and papers in the books and academic journals of the past three decades. Thus, all the observations I make are circumscribed by my own limitations as a perpetual student of the field who is not even a professional academic, and some of them will seem less useful or relevant to those from other cultures and/or alternative linguistic traditions.

Only two decades ago, trans studies books and papers were relatively infrequent occurrences. But the days are now long gone when any one person not named *Stryker* could hope to have familiarity with the full breadth of the field as it has developed. Much of this can be credited both to the hard work of trans academics and of *Transgender Studies Quarterly (TSQ)*, which has ignited interest in trans theory in ways I doubt anyone fully anticipated.

In any case, I realize it is impossible to make accurate statements about any academic endeavor that has grown as broad as trans studies, and one which is increasingly international, multicultural, and multilingual in scope. On the one hand, any generalization is open to attack for its imprecision by pointing to what it leaves out; but the alternative—to refuse to characterize the field—renders critique impossible.

To paraphrase from Andrea Long Chu's observation by about feminism: *Trans studies is defined by its refusal of trans as a coherent or finished category, on the grounds that it remains permanently incomplete. This has put theorists of transgender in the unenviable position of being politically obligated to defend its impossibility: in order to be* for *transgender people, we must refrain from making any positive claims* about *transgender people. The result is a kind of negative theology, dedicated to striking down the graven images of a god whose stated preference for remaining beyond comprehensive description has left those worshipping her up in the air.*[1]

Yet writing a book that speaks directly to transgender people and trans studies forces me into contradicting both Chu and Radi, while making an alarming number of affirmative statements and declarations about transgender people, especially in terms of what author Gabriel Mac memorably termed "mindfuck shitshow of transitioning."[2]

I do this knowing that there are important exceptions to every assertion I make. Nonetheless, the only alternative is to continually interrupt the reader with reminders of all the exceptions to whatever has just been written, or simply not to make such assertions at all.

In choosing not to do this, I realize I inevitably obscure significant swaths of trans community. I hope they will forgive me and seek revenge by writing better and more representative books than I have been able to.

A Word About Language

This book focuses mostly on transgender women, in particular transsexual women and others who—because of feelings of gender dysphoria or their deeply felt desires—seek to change their bodies' primary and secondary sexual characteristics. First, because doing so follows Mark Twain's advice to "write what you know." But second, because I simply have no other firsthand experience as a trans person and I'm not so presumptuous as to assume I can write accurately about others—such as trans males or nonbinary individuals. Having said this, I also don't imagine I speak for anything like a majority of trans women, not only because of my personal limitations as a white, privileged person, but especially in a book that is as much personal as it is theoretical.

I am also significantly older and had my surgery much longer ago than the majority of trans women alive today, which similarly circumscribes my experiences and thinking. I'm sure many other women, especially those who are non-op, pre-op, or fortunate enough to receive blockers and hormones in adolescence and have had very different experiences, would offer very different thoughts on these topics. Despite such significant limitations to the subject position from which I write, I still often use "we," and I hope readers will forgive this convenient shorthand as an authorial conceit rather than an attempt to speak for everyone.

I have also generally not addressed the experiences and epistemic challenges posed by crossdressers in any depth, although they are certainly central to the transgender family. I realize this is a common failing across trans studies, which does not make it right.

If I have focused mostly on trans women who have had surgery, it is also because this is an area I know something about from the inside, and this is the area where I have struggled most personally. In addition, I believe postoperative bodies and embodiment represent some of the most profound breaks with cisgender understanding of sex and bodies, as well as the strongest challenges to both our visual knowledge of gender and to our sense of bodily aesthetics.

When illustrating a point about sexuality, I have also used fairly binary examples of man/woman/ masculine/feminine in most places to emphasize a point about sexuality for simplicity's sake, simply because we tend to understand sexuality in very binary ways. This is not to promote the idea that sex must be binary, much less to promote the idea of transnormativity, which—as Florence Ashley correctly notes—"privileges trans men and women to the detriment of others . . . elevating a narrow conception of transitude based on its proximity to hegemonic gender ideology."[3]

I use terms like "cis," "cisgender," "cissociety," and "cisculture" to refer broadly to those who are not transgender. In multiple places, I criticize the oppression inflicted on trans people by cisgender cultures. Yet, I know that any generalization about an enormous and complex population risks being generally accurate but deeply flawed. Mine are no different, but there is no room here to go into longer explanations of the diversity available among cisgender people. Suffice it to say, there are many cisgender people who are as committed to gender rights as any trans person—some even more so—and that many continue to do important work building out the study of gender and defending the lives of transgender people. More than a few are cited in this book.

As theorist/activist Cathy Cohen reminds us about heteronormativity and heterosexual culture, there is no uniform cisgender culture from which all cisgender people benefit.[4] Since sex is itself deeply structured through raced, classed, abled, and colonial matrices, there are many bodies within cisculture that are abjected in ways that are highly similar to transgender people's. On the other hand, there are certainly many transgender people who hold deeply reactionary and regressive views about gender and/or sex.

In writing of intersex people, I note that some are increasingly using Differences of Sexual Development or DSD (which itself replaced Disorders of Sexual Development). It has become an alternative identification used by many such individuals. Some DSD-identified individuals feel that intersex is stigmatizing or that what they have is a condition rather than an identity, while some intersex-identified people feel that what they have is not a medical condition but a normal variation, that intersex claims a community and a history, and/or by focusing on disorders, they can better engage the medical field in proving improving care for affected infants. Because of the variety of opinions on this topic, for simplicity's sake, I've continued to used either "intersex" or "intersex/DSD" here—but certainly all such people have the right to define the name under which they are recognized.

I have used trans and transgender more or less interchangeably throughout, which for me imply a category that remains perpetually open to change new identities as they announce themselves. As theorist Blas Radi notes,

> There have been attempts to subsume them under a single category by proposing "umbrella terms," but there seem to be as many umbrellas as there are terms. . . . Trans [is] not a way of homogenizing the specificities that distinguish these (and many more) categories from one another, but rather a way of evoking a multiplicity that is not limited to trans women and men [and] includes all those identities whereby a person does not identify with the gender they were assigned at birth.[5]

The sheer diversity of those now sheltering under the well-worn "transgender umbrella" is a challenge for any author hoping to write accurately about them. A 2023 *Washington Post*/KFF poll of adults found that only 31 percent of those identifying as transgender or trans had undergone any kind of medical care.[6] I have used transsexual when speaking specifically of this sub-minority of the trans community who transition to bodies that they understand as being those of men and women.

With that said, I recognize that not all those who undergo medical transition and surgery identify under that label, see themselves as "changing sexes," or even see themselves as either women or men. In fact, a 2022 Pew Research poll of Gen Z (ages eighteen to twenty-nine) found that among those who identify as "trans," only 40 percent identify within such simple binary categories as "trans boy" or "trans girl"—a development that would have been impossible to predict when I transitioned in 1978.[7]

Riki Wilchins

2024

ACKNOWLEDGMENTS

Many thanks to Abraham Weil and Katharine Jenkins, both of whom were kind enough to read an early draft of this book and make many patient and insightful suggestions on how it might be improved.

1

How to (Not) Talk About (Trans) Sex

"What We're Rollin' Around in Bed With"

Why can't the erotic be a site of producing trans identity or practices?[1]

—ADAIR AND AIZURA ("'THE TRANSGENDER CRAZE SEDUCING OUR [SONS]'; OR, ALL THE TRANS GUYS ARE JUST DATING EACH OTHER," TRANSGENDER STUDIES QUARTERLY)

There's so little appreciation for the knowledge that can come with arousal.[2]

—FLORENCE ASHLEY (GENDER/FUCKING: PLEASURES AND POLITICS OF LIVING IN A GENDERED BODY)

For some time now, I have wrestled with how to write about the twin issues of trans sexuality and erotic embodiment about which trans studies, for all its demonstrable intellectual brilliance, is still largely silent.

It's an especially pressing question for those of us for whom sexuality and gender are radically inseparable, as Billy Huff explains:

> I inject testosterone into my thighs every other week in the hopes of being railed by an anonymous fag in the backroom of a bar. . . . I cannot think my gender without recourse to my sexuality. . . . According to hegemonic trends in Transgender Studies . . . I am mistaken at best, and at worst, I am an impossibility. Gender and sexuality are commonly maintained as separate phenomena that emerge from distinct ontological and epistemological foundations . . . [but this] separation of gender and sexuality is not a necessary or sufficient condition for transness.[3]

In their groundbreaking essay, *Who We Rollin' Around in Bed With: Sexual Silences in Feminism*, Amber Hollibaugh and Cherríe Moraga lamented "this most privatized aspect of ourselves, our sex lives, has dead-ended into silence."[4] They were speaking of and to 1980s feminism, but the observation applies still rings true about today about trans studies.

The "who" in their essay were the figures of "politically incorrect" lesbian sex—the suppressed desires of femmes for butches and butches for femmes, for gender roles and sex acts suffused lust and the power dynamics of dominance, desire, and submission that were considered politically inconvenient, even "oppressive to women," and were thus sentenced to academic silence.

But I'm more interested in the "what" of sex, and the long-suppressed exploration of the transgender body, its pleasures, its desires, and how we inhabit and experience it (or fail to) during sexual intimacy. It is no coincidence that these are the very challenges that have consumed much of my own thinking these past forty-five years.

While queer studies has tended to reduce the body to a text upon which things are written and read, trans studies has tended to reduce it to a site of dysphoria and identity.

Certainly, there have been a small but remarkable stable of writers who have addressed trans sexuality and/or erotic embodiment at times: C. Jacob Hale's *Leatherdyke Boys and Their Daddies: How To Have Sex Without Men or Women*; Morty Diamond's anthology *Trans/Love: Radical Sex, Love & Relationships Beyond the Gender Binary*; Susan Stryker's *Dungeon Intimacies: The Poetics of Transsexual Sadomasochism*, and, of course less recently, the diaries of the late Lou Sullivan.[5,6,7,8] Since 2020, theorist Billy Huff has centered trans sexuality (and its elision from trans theory) in a trio of remarkable articles and chapters.[9,10]

There is also an expanding number of nontheoretical books focused on trans erotica like Florence Ashley's personal tour of sex, *Gender/Fucking: the Pleasures and Politics of Living in a Gendered Body*, erotic anthologies like *Nerve Endings: The New Trans Erotic*, and any frequent online pieces published by digital publications like *Autostraddle*.[11,12,13]

On embodiment, legendary academics like Talia Mae Bettcher, Eric Prosser, and Gayle Salamon have all developed deeply considered philosophical explorations. Although not analytical, Trystan Cotten's pioneering anthologies—*Below the Belt* and *Hung Jury*—feature trans men speaking candidly about their genitals and related surgeries. However, none of these really address the intersection of bodies, erotics, and sexuality.[14,15] Elijah Edelman and Lal Zimman's *Boycunts and Bonus Holes: Trans Men's Bodies, Neoliberalism, and the Sexual Productivity of Genitals* goes much farther in this direction, exploring the erotic and linguistic practices of trans men within the constraints imposed by anatomy, surgical technique, cisnormative language, and neoliberal sensibilities.[16]

It seems notable that may of the authors in this (admittedly incomplete) list are transgender men. One is tempted to make the ironical observation that, as a learning community, trans academia is unconsciously replicating the hoary gender stereotype that every man wants to talk about *his* junk but no lady ever wants to talk about *hers*.

This is facile, but it would certainly explain why a well-published trans male scholar recently pointed out to me that he and other trans men regularly discuss the sex they're having, but—while I've known hundreds of trans women—I can recall exactly *none* of them ever mentioning sex. Nor did I, for that matter.[17]

Perhaps this is because trans women's eroticism is so highly politicized; delighting in our girldicks risks being labeled as "male energy," while delighting in vaginal embodiment risks our being labeled as self-arousing fetishists.

Trans male eroticism is politicized along somewhat different axes. I don't presume to speak for trans men, but anyone who follows the literature can find feminist, queer, and sometimes even transmasculine discourse on the trans male body that is deeply tethered to cisnormative ideals, or which mines the nasty outdates trope of the "Failed Phallus" (an epistemic violence in its own right). Such writing is particularly egregious from lesbian feminist academics who should know better.

As one prominent scholar—who had written yet another restrained scholarly article defending the trans male phallus—wrote to me:

[P]eople writing about SRS with no personal experience of their own seems incredibly presumptuous. These theorists are invested in a discourse of failed GAS (Gender Affirming Surgery) for trans men, because it jives with queer deconstructions of masculinity/ maleness as an endlessly deferred and unattainable concept. The thing that really kills me is the use of cisgender men's bodies as the norm for judging trans men's bodies. These theorists know better than that; they're not that stupid. They're very aware of the language they use, and it's purposeful. It's been so hard for me to do this article, it's very emotional, which makes it hard to do my best writing.[18]

And of course, genitalia and genital sex tends to be the one thing to which cisgender theorists and the cisgender public are happy to reduce transgender (and intersex) people—what legal scholar Grabham has termed "hyper-embodiment."[19] As Natalie Reed points out in the "The Eunuch, The Rapist, The Whore And The Child Who Simply Knew," cisworld has always offered severely limited menu of options for understanding or thinking, much less theorizing about, transgender sexuality.[20]

Cisgender society obsesses over our genitalia, sensationalizing what we have in our underwear, passing law after law on the legal implications of the lack or presence of specific genital formations, so that the states in half the country have now made a synecdoche for gender. We are perhaps the only minority in history whose genital area and their associated activities have been subject to such exhaustive media attention, public debate, legislative initiatives, and medico/academic discourse.

Even worse, cisgender society has used our sexuality against us as a primary means of oppression by medical systems: "trans people who report eroticizing their natal genitals or who articulate sexual desire as part of their need to transition regularly risk being denied care. Outside of such systems, we have been cast as evil deceivers, sex perverts, groomers and predators."[21] And this kind of vile sexualized slur is often particularly common in attacks on our most vulnerable: young women of color or those who are incarcerated.

So some might naturally ask: Why add fuel to this bonfire of libels by writing about the fact that as trans people we have sex, like sex, struggle with sex, and sometimes lose ourselves in sex?

Talking frankly and personally about our sexuality and erotic embodiment is fraught for writers in the academy in other ways as well.

After all, having sex is not a topic about which PhD committees are eagerly searching for dissertations, nor a field of study for which promotion committees are chomping at the bit to grant tenure.

As theorist Susan Stryker has noted, in almost any system of thought, "no place is shunted to the periphery of consideration with greater alacrity than is the body."[22] Sex is considered a kind of second-class cousin to respectable research and theorization, only slightly more reputable than studying phrenology or UFOs.

And of course, there is the sad existence of an entire cottage industry of TERF academics ready to exploit any exploration of trans women's sexuality as fetishizing "real" female bodies or even—according to some theories—fetishizing our own: the perfect definition of a double-bind.

Moreover, we must always shunt our own sexuality to the side when writing for peer-reviewed journals of PhD committees. A sure way to render any paper suspect is to admit that it deals with something that personally aroused its author. Arousal is vaguely disputable, a kind of "kinks," a failure to maintain objectivity by allowing desire or arousal to intrude. This supposedly undermines the very scholarly distance which is the hallmark of academic writing, poisoning the claim of objectivity and serious investigation.

Confessing to being aroused by the "wrong" kind of desire opens one to be categorized as having what used to be called a "perversion," and is now more politely termed as "paraphilia." Even having the "right" kind of desire—if it is deemed "too" strong—makes one vulnerable to accusations of having the many-dreaded "fetishistic desires." This phrase is reminiscent of the pro-sex lesbian feminists' description of porn: "Porn is the erotica you like, while porn is the erotica you *don't* like." Similarly, normal eroticism are the kinks of which society approves, while fetishistic eroticism are the kinks of which *disapproves*. If I'm a guy who gets a raging hard-on from putting on leather and studs, I'm a regular guy; if I have the same reaction to putting on a French maid uniform and 5-inch heels, I'm a pervert.

Moreover, as theorist Julia Serano has observed, sex itself is stigmatized in our culture, and, as a result, people who are seen as "marked by sex" are derided, delegitimized, and demonized. Which is why sexualization is such a powerful tool for invalidating nearly anything or anyone.[23] Especially marginalized groups, who are either excessively de-sexed in society's eyes (such as people with disabilities) or perceived as "excessively" sexual (gay or trans people, colonized populations, people of color, those in lower-income levels, etc.) Male members of such groups are stereotyped as "predators" and females as "promiscuous"—there is no healthy desire or eroticism that dare speak its name, and certainly not any subaltern sort of *kink*.

Psychiatry, queer politics, academic prejudice, and weaponization by cissociety generally and TERFs specifically have made sex a minefield for any academic seeking to study it with anything like the serious attention afforded to its close cousin, gender.

Also, for many of trans people, sexuality also engages the subject of abuse. As I wrote in *Read My Lips*, trans children often present the ideal profile for sexual predators: we tend to be socially awkward and isolated, emotionally transparent, desperate for adult approval, out of touch with our bodies, confused about our sexuality, and *used to keeping secrets about our bodies*. If there is a predatory shark swimming in the water nearby, the social thrashing of a genderqueer kid is bound to attract them.

And of course, any exploration of transgender sexuality and erotic embodiment involves delving into the effects of gender-affirming genital surgical procedures, which—as *TSQ's Surgery Issue* drily noted—"is talked about mostly to remind people not to talk about it so much."[24]

An Underprivileged Site of Inquiry

The silence in trans studies around trans sexuality is all the more striking given its provenance in queer theory. Scholars like David Eng noted as far back as 2005 that queer theory has always understood sexuality to be a *privileged* site of critical attention.[25] Yet despite the logic of this now-common observation, I would argue that exactly the opposite has actually been true.

Queer theory has surely theorized the *concept* of sexuality as it relates to heteronormativity in enormous detail—by which they mean one's sexual orientation. But of queer sexuality itself, it has offered almost nothing other than clinical studies about frequency, dysfunction, and so on.[26]

In my own cursory investigation of a distinctly nonrandom sample of three of the better-known "legacy" gay studies journals—the *Journal of Homosexuality, Journal of Lesbian Studies,* and *GLQ*—I could find no articles devoted to critical analyses of acts like anal intercourse, oral sex, or even anything with words like "strap-on," "dildo," or "fisting," and so on—let alone actual practice or personal experience.

When it comes to queer/trans academia, apparently anal sex is not deviant enough for consideration, not something normative gay men or women (or queer trans people) do, or simply not something worthy of academic interrogation. Who would have guessed?[27]

To find such articles, one has to turn to journals like the *Archives of Sexual Behavior, Journal of Sex, Sexuality and Culture,* and so on.

Yet the legacy gay studies journals I search were replete with papers reinterpreting gay sexuality across different time periods, through different types of media (books, film, TV), and across the entire geography of Eurocentric colonization—often all three at once— especially through its textual reinterpretation.

A prototypical tasty gay journal title might read something like: "Colonial Depictions of 'Sodomy' among Indigenous Sub-Saharan Peoples in 15th Century European Literature: a Reconsideration." It is no wonder that the first *New York Times* mention of queer theory would identify it as "a prism through which scholars examine literary texts."[28] Needless to say, all of this is at a safe academic distance from anything to do with the sticky physicality of actual gay sex.

Even when a loaded topic like anal or oral sex *was* the subject of an article, it was comfortably deflected onto subaltern populations, such as queers of color, HIV positive individuals, and ethnic subcultures—as if this was something that diverged from mainstream gay practice.

For example, the first and *only* title with "anal sex" I found in any issue of *GLQ* online was "Black Anality"—although it is safe to assume that more than more than one confused white boy has indulged in the practice as well—perhaps when he was drunk late at night and didn't fully realize what he was doing until the morning after. The *Journal of Lesbian and Gay Studies* and *Journal of Homosexuality* were not much better in this regard: the only articles I could find on anal sex were studies of HIV.

Notably, when the journal *Social Text* devoted an entire 2005 double issue to the idea of queer studies moving *away* from an exclusive focus on sexuality as a privileged site of inquiry, not a single article was actually *about* sex. Chapter titles about bodies, shame, castration, and so on looked promising but contained virtually nothing about actual sexual practice, bodies, arousal, or erotic pleasure.

The study of queerness has morphed into the ontological state of *being* queer, detached from any queer sexual acts in which queer bodies might engage. Desire is a little more than an abstraction, a concept, a field of semantic interest that never smells of the sweat of bodies in heat.

Yet as former *TSQ* editor Susan Striker explained, what first drew her to queer theory was the blazing hope that it would "rupture the foundational containers of desire to release a raw erotic power which could be harnessed for a radical social agenda."[29] The reality has turned out a little differently.

Trans sexuality has not fared much better. Filipo Maria Nimbi et al. explain that "Having a healthy and pleasurable sexual life can be challenging for transgender individuals [yet] few studies have attempted to understand transgender people's sexual needs nor their desire to achieve a more satisfying sexual experience."[30] In conducting their own exhaustive literature search of articles on transgender sexual desire and fantasies, Nimbi et al. were unable to find a single "available study in the literature which focused on the transgender population."

Presumably, the bulk of the studies examined were from cisgender academics, but trans academics have also not pursued Styker's vision of an "anti-oedipal, ecstatic leap . . . in which the foundational containers of desire could be ruptured to release a raw erotic power."[31] She writes hopefully that trans studies will "follow its own . . . to address the critical study of gender and sexuality, identity, embodiment, and desire in ways that gay, lesbian, and queer studies have not always successfully managed."[32]

But as far as I can tell, we are still awaiting the joyous anti-oedipal leap which might ignite such study. For example, as the preeminent academic journal in the field and still the only one devoted to trans studies, *TSQ* devoted its inaugural issue to eighty-six alphabetically organized essays on trans embodiment. But it skipped from *Gender Self-Determination* to *Guerilla* without ever mentioning, ummm . . . *Genitals*—which would seem a pretty strong candidate for inclusion in any discussions of trans embodiment.[33]

It also jumped from *Revolution* right to *Sick* without ever mentioning *Sex*. Tantalizingly, there was an essay devoted to *Hips*, but it made no mention of the organs most associated with hips or what function hips tend to perform during intimacy.

And while TSQ's "*Surgery Issue*" masterfully interrogated the arguments advanced to justify trans surgeries, the "discourse of distress" which gatekeepers still often expect, the problems of accessing surgery in Brazil, and the problems of getting labiaplasty, it had nothing about how this most intimate of body modification might affect trans people's erotic embodiment, arousal, pleasure, or sexual functioning. If anything, trans academia's *ecstatic leap* has been used to jump right over sexuality to nearly anything it can address on the other side except its own *raw erotic power*.

In fact, like nearly every other academic publication I've seen which has dwelt on the subject of medical transition, the issue contained nothing about sex itself—before *or* after surgery. Even a *TSQ* issue devoted to porn featured academic interrogation of the industry but little about the actual sex in which trans actors' engage.

As T. Cooper writes in his quasi-memoir, *Real Man Adventures*:[34] HER: Hey, are you going to write about sex in your book?ME: Hey, are you fucking kidding me?HER: That's what people always want to know about.ME: No fucking way.HER: Just asking . . . The late Mira Bellwether rightfully complains in her exuberantly obscene 'zine *Fucking Trans Women* that "We deserve to have sex without it becoming a gender studies class."[35] She's right, but I would add that we also deserve to have our sex at least be *mentioned* in a trans studies class . . . or in a publication.

Since the editorial staff of trans studies' leading journal tends to allow issue topics to *bubble up* from the academic community, this elision of sex, erotic embodiment, or romantic intimacy—despite their being key issues in nearly every transgender person's life and transition—says perhaps less about the publication itself, and unacknowledged silences among trans academics as a whole, and perhaps the wider community as well. Billy Huff reports that when he posted online about transitioning to have sex as a *fag*, he was roundly attacked for not taking transitions seriously, devaluing the transitions of others, and conflating gender identity with sexuality.[36]

A Language of Erotic Aesthetics

[T]ransgender studies focuses on the examination and theorization of non-normative genders,

    and queer studies assesses and analyzes non-normative sexualities.[37]

    —CÁEL KEEGAN ("TRANSGENDER STUDIES, OR HOW TO
    DO THINGS WITH TRANS")

My aim is to open more discursive space for considerations of trans- fantasies and sexuality and to argue that it is crucial for us to pay more critical attention to fantasies and their fulfillment in our consideration of what it means to be trans-, indeed, what it means to become a gendered and sexual body at all.[38]

    —BILLY HUFF ("ON [BE]COMING IN BOYSTOWN")

Writer Andrea Long Chu critiqued queer studies by observing that "trying to study sexuality without studying gender would be manifestly absurd."[39] I would argue that trans studies is doing the reverse—trying to study gender without studying sexuality. Yet gender is inextricably intertwined with both sexuality and embodiment.

In "Thinking Sex," Gayle Rubin famously noted that however much sexuality and gender are related experiences, "they form the basis of two distinct arenas of social practice."[40] But I'm not so sure.

How does this map onto complex identities, such as that depicted in the queer classic, "Stone Butch Blues," where Leslie Feinberg's protagonist *Jess* is both transmasculine and a lesbian?[41] More recently, in "Wanting Bad Things" Andrea Long Chu talks about the impossibility of separating her transsexuality from her desire for other women.[42] In "On [Be]Coming in Boystown," Huff writes about his transness as arising directly from his lifelong desire to be a trans fag having anonymous hot sex with men.[43]

We are aroused by the thought of muscular arms or rounded hips, or excited by the sensations of kissing a soft cheek or a stubbly five o'clock shadow. The shapely curve or the muscular jut of a buttock or chest or soft breast or buttock catch our eyes on the street.

Not that sexual attraction and erotic embodiment have to be this dimorphic. As a nonbinary writer, R. E. Wallace complains about the interlocking semiotics of dimorphic gender with sexuality:

The message I receive from culture is that my transness, my masculinity, and perhaps most of all my ambiguity, exclude me from "hotness. . . ." [T]here can be no truly "gender neutral" sexiness, and that elements of masculine and feminine sexiness are seen to cancel each other out; embodying both at once is impossible. Desirability is made a function of intense sexual dimorphism: large breasts on soft-faced, hairless women, or heavy musculature on stubbly men with chiseled jaws.[44]

Despite the fact that we tend to theorize them separately as Rubin suggested, it may actually be impossible to *think* gendered identities or gendered expressions completely divorced from ideas of sexuality and arousal.[45]

Or from sexual orientation. As Bettcher explains, "[S]exual orientation is not merely determined by stable gendered 'object preference,'" but also "includes a core erotic gendered self," blurring "the traditional distinction between gender identity and sexual orientation."[46]

In many ways, gender is the public expression of the sexed body. We are attracted to others or assess them as potential sexual partners based on their gender expression. Gender is among the ways we seek to arouse desire in potential partners. What could masculinity and femininity, or being a woman or man, signify apart from the sexed body?

It is a fact that gender is inextricably embedded in a matrix of arousal, and erotic aesthetics that make gender displays so highly meaningful, and results in changing genders so tightly regulated. The idea of "changing sexes" doesn't just upset cis people morally or politically, but aesthetically and sexually as well.

The semiotics of gender—both its outer expressions and in the body itself—are built around a language of sexual aesthetics. A gay man in Levis and leather and showing a spray of chest hair as he cruises the Castro is not just "expressing his gender identity" but also expressing his sense of erotic embodiment and communicating a complex sexual semiotics to possible partners.

Back when I was trying feverishly to pass—meaning high heels, makeup, long hair, and a dress—I was deploying a visual language that, intentionally or not, presented me as an object of potential male heterosexual attraction. And transphobic male mouth breathers on the subway responded to this presentation by either snickering and pointing to show that they knew I was "really a guy" and they were not taken in or giving me that long, intrusive gaze and then getting pissed when they realized I was "really a guy" and they had unintentionally and momentarily considered me a feminine sexual object.

When we assert that all trans women *are* women, we are also implicitly (and sometimes explicitly) declaring the transfem penis or *girldick* to be female body part, and thus a femininely gendered organ. This is obviously a huge leap for many, perhaps most, people—not just epistemically but also aesthetically in terms of their erotic sensibility of the female body. But our many analyses of trans abjection and cis-centrism usually ignore this, even though this connection is pretty obvious to all involved, and thus remain radically incomplete.

Phantasmagorical Pleasures

As one of the two founding texts of queer theory, *Gender Trouble* contains scores of mentions of "desire" and "pleasure," but none of actual sex—other than to point out its "phantasmagorical nature."[47] I mean, I've actually *had* sex a couple times, and "phantasmagorical" was not the first word that sprung to my mind (although that is probably less true for my partners). The book also mentions "pleasure" seventy-five times, but actual "intercourse" only once. And it mentions "genitalia" only three or four times, all in relation to the constructedness of sex. We learn nothing about what genitals do, how they feel, or how either might be affected by this constructedness.

To me such omissions were especially perplexing, because Butler was among the small core of sex-positive theorists whose exploration of lesbian sexuality at Barnard College's infamous 1983 Conference on Sexuality ignited a firestorm of protest from anti-sex and anti-porn feminists which became known as the Lesbian Sex Wars. It was an intellectual and political confrontation that would consume much of feminist academia during the following decade (more on this in a moment).[48]

Yet despite the Sex Wars and its intensive foregrounding of sexuality as a site of feminist investment, as lesbian theory merged into queer theory, sex was once again pushed to the intellectual sidelines—inevitably critical theory's unwanted stepchild.

Gender Trouble is thus a prime exemplar of the field it helped bring into being: one in which desire, pleasure, embodiment, and sex as disembodied abstractions that function as placeholders for whatever larger post-structuralist argument is being advanced—conceptual gestures toward something not meant in the literal sense and meriting the kind of serious scholarly attention afforded things like power or discourse.[49]

This avoidance of sexuality and embodiment represents a kind of politics in its own right, an extension of queer theory's tendency to dehumanize the subject, which it sees as little more than the sum and surface of the discourses in which it is embedded. Because real subjects, who are not strictly discursive in nature but who struggle with the vicissitudes of their flesh and are possessed of sufficient agency to deploy it in erotic encounters and experience its pleasures, are things that queer theory wants to avoid. Queer theory is interested in the Body, but not our bodies; in the discursive construction of genitals, but not the literal construction of trans genitals; in Sexuality, but not in our having sex or our sexual pleasures.

It is queer theory's own philosophic posture that imposes these limits, causing it to largely elide the ways that desire and pleasure are also affected by discourse, are integral to subjectivity, and create potential sites for queer resistance.[50] Yet as embodied subjects, we have no choice but to engage with and to wrestle with these bodies and this constructedness every time we engage in intimacy. And this is even more true for those of us whose literal construction of our bodies makes it a constant site for contestation, politicization, and semiotic instability.

Interestingly, *Gender Trouble* mentions "vagina" only twice but "penis" nearly a dozen times, even devoting an entire chapter to the *faux* signifier of the Lacanian (here lesbian) "phallus" of sex/gender. It might have been both more informative and disruptive of prevailing tropes had Butler deconstructed the discourse around the vagina as an organ of loathing, lack, and absence. Instead, *Gender Trouble* unconsciously reiterates hetero culture's relentless insistence that the Penis is the sole substance and signifier of Sex.

This observation parallels my own personal experience. In the nearly half-century I've been verbally prodded and poked by scores of cisgender people about my transition and/or surgery, *not one person* has ever asked me about *gaining a vagina*—although this was clearly the reason for my own bottom surgery—not even lesbians, whom one would imagine have some personal experience with the appeal of this organ.

Instead, every single dialog about bottom surgery has been framed around *losing a penis* because in phallocentric societies (which is to say almost all of them), as the visible, extruded synecdoche for both Sex and Gender, it is the only genital that matters; or as theorist Eric Plemons put it more elegantly, "the presence of a phallus is the single strongest signifier of sex on a body . . . its removal is, therefore, more important than its replacement."[51]

Decrying and deconstructing phallogocentric discourse is not the same as theorizing alternative epistemologies. Thus, *Gender Trouble* leaves the reader wondering in vain what a genuinely vaginocentric signifying economy might look like, what kinds of discourses it might enable, and what kinds of signifying practices it would enable or foreclose.

But as always, we are inevitably left with the Penis. Within *Gender Trouble*'s own unconscious unintentional phallogocentrism, a reflection of the larger culture's, in which the vagina remains absence, emptiness, lack, nothing—and nobody needs nothing. And more importantly, nobody can *interrogate* nothing.

Down the Rabbit Hole

If queer theory has tended to theorize gender while avoiding saying much about how it interacts with desire and pleasure, deconstructing the gender system and gendered subjectivity while offering little about the how such subjects might experience their sexuality or gendered eroticism, it is a rabbit hole down which that trans studies has followed.

Sexual orientation, gender, gender identity, body image, arousal—all of these are intertwined in complex ways that our theory seldom fully acknowledges. Giving a full account of genders, nonnormative or otherwise, will mean engaging in what it means to have sex, to inhabit a sexed body, and to experience it during arousal and pleasure.

At first, Chu's widely read *New York Times* op-ed "My New Vagina Won't Make Me Happy (It Shouldn't Have To")" appeared to be a welcome and notable exception.[52] But despite the promising title, it repeatedly foregrounded her future vagina's expected *failure* to bestow happiness or pleasure, and the intimate pain she anticipated from dilation—while saying nothing about any *joys* it might enable or any intimate *pleasures* from penetrations of other sorts that her new vagina-to-be might make possible.

According to the piece, trans vaginas are merely a massive disappointment-in-waiting, with "no good outcomes" and women not "begging" for sex or pleasure but "be to taken seriously." What a drag. I read it begging for her to take the sexuality of her own vagina-to-be seriously. How could it *make her happy* if she never intends to take it out to play?

Here, sexuality is not just unmentioned, but has been pushed entirely off the stage. The trans woman is here reduced to her gender, completely neutered. It is a perfect synopsis of trans theory's engagement with the sexed body and trans eroticism. And as with the so-called "Failed Phallus" discourse among some lesbian academics, no writer who doesn't actually *have* a vagina should be pontificating about what they will or won't do for them. Mark Twain may be widely quoted for advising aspiring authors to "Write what you know"—but somewhat less quoted is the second part of his admonition: "and stick with organs you actually *own*."

For many trans people, not only gender identity but also sexuality are integral to transition, hormones, and surgery. An academic who had lived his life as a "gold-star" butch with zero interest in men told me how once he transitioned, "Suddenly all the parts and the power dynamics *just lined up*." He became a gay man who is exclusively attracted to other men.[53] His self-identification *as* a trans gay man flowed from his sexuality, his body, *and* his gender identification.

What makes such stories all the more extraordinary is that for decades now we have understood sexual orientation as fixed from birth and unchangeable. Apparently not for some of us (a fact that no one seems to have examined). And of course there's Huff, whose transition was to fulfill his lifelong desire for gay sex with men—or as he puts it bluntly: "My gender identity is trans-fag bottom boy."[54]

All of this shows how transgender, and perhaps gender identity, cannot be cleanly separated from sexuality.

Even the erotic acts we perform are themselves heavily gendered, from the gender dynamics of "pitchers" versus "catchers" in penetrative sex, to way we gender the organs (or sex toys) involved. It is virtually impossible to imagine any sex act which is not in some way constructed as highly gendered.[55] Even solo masturbation often engages overtones of gender. And for those trans people who change our bodies, we quickly realize that trans isn't just a gendered identity but a sexual one that provides new erotic possibilities.

Some influential trans scholars have suggested we use trans* with an asterisk, to show its openness, and to think of the category as *symbolizing radiant, multipronged means and methods of entrainment—a virtual potential immanent within processes of* *materialization . . . through movements, connections, intensifications, and refigurations that traverse existing material arrangements.*

Nowhere in such an expansive definition is sexuality or embodiment mentioned. Not all of us want gender-affirming surgeries. But surely among those of us who do, one reason is not only aligning our bodies with our gendered identities but also because we want those bodies to *do* specific things with others and to have others do specific things *to* them. That is to say, one can only hope that one day, with all those processes transversing materialities and movements, the field might traverse its way to finally interrogating our radiant, multiple prongs doing some intensified *wanking off.*

"Our Right to Mainstream"

The historical figure of the Homosexual had always had at least two characteristics which made him (the Homosexual was nearly always male) "queer." He lacked a normative masculine gender expression and displayed traditionally feminine qualities, and he also lacked a normative—that is, hetero—sexuality. He engaged in a variety of activities contained under that notorious label: sodomy—an ill-defined moral, religious, and legal category which could and did encompass anything from felatio and cunnilingus to bestiality and buggery.

Socially, sodomy was considered a *crime against nature*, religiously it was a *mortal sin*, and legally a was a criminal offense. Needless to say, such acts, when performed between two men were the very definition of deviant and generally masculine behavior. The line between gender and sexuality, never very clear, was completely erased when it came to queer sex.

An emerging homophile movement, seeking to make itself more acceptable to the public, began to rebrand the Homosexual, discarding everything that made it both queer and a homosexual.

First to go was the Homosexual's sexuality. Mainstream gay discourse began erasing any reference to sex in regard to gay people: digital, anal, or oral sex—all of it had to go.

Even desiring sex was purged, and disappearing under a massive rebranding campaign that recast gay desire as a soulful, if neutered, romantic *love*—as in "Who We Love," which was amended to "Our Right to Love," before finally being condensed to the simple, if tautological, "Love Is Love." No one was to ever heard promoting slogans like "Our Right to Fellate" or "Buggery Is Buggery."

As sexuality disappeared from discourse *about* gays, there was still the problem of the Homosexual's deviant gender: that was next to go.

As George Chauncy recalls in "Gay New York: Gender, Urban Culture, and the Making of the Gay Male World": "'[F]airies' (homosexual men who displayed feminine or effeminate characteristics) were spurned by mainly white, middle-class, gay men who developed subjectivities based on a gender-normative understanding of their same-sex desire."[56] It was only in the early decades of the twentieth century, from perhaps the 1930s through the 1950s, that this

> now-conventional division of men into "homosexuals" and "heterosexuals," based on the sex of their sexual partners, replaced the division of men into "fairies" and "normal" men as the basis of their imaginary gender status as the hegemonic way of

understanding sexuality. Moreover, the transition from one sexual regime to the next was an uneven process, marked by significant class and ethnic differences.

As Paisley Currah explains, "[T]hese neat definitional boxes are artifacts of a twentieth-century class antagonism between feminine 'fairies' and masculine 'queers.' This history is obscured by the contemporary policing of categories and the incentives of identity politics, which tries to contain the messiness of desire and gender by permanently assigning everyone their own letter in the LGBT acronym."[57]

By the 1970s, largely middle- and upper-class, urban white gay men who had long chafed under stereotypes of homosexuals as all artsy, fey, and effeminate began manning up and beefing up, flooding into gyms and spawning an entire culture of muscular, macho gay "clone" styles like the *muscle queen, the leatherman*, and so on. Rather than offering a new set of terms for manhood, these sought instead to read gayness into acceptable stereotypes of white, working-class, hetero hypermasculinity.

Gay masculinity became commodified as a set of recognizable and highly stylized "types." The 1970s hit group *The Village People* was the apotheosis of this, with its ripped, openly gay members each performing as a specific macho straight male archetype—*the cop, the cowboy, the construction worker*, and so on—while singing cheeky songs like, "Macho Macho Man," "Y.M.C.A," and "In the Navy" that both winked at straight audiences and invited them to be in on the joke.

Eventually both sexual practice and gender deviance were erased from gay *and* mainstream discourse. Henceforth, recognizing the butchness of some lesbian women or the effeminacy of some gay men in polite company would be viewed as outdated, perhaps even homophobic, stereotyping. Today, not a single national and state gay rights organization mentions masculinity among lesbian women or femininity among gay men on the websites or in their materials. It was as dead as disco.

While such genderqueer gays still existed, it was only for annual Gay Pride Parades when drag queens and *Dykes on Bikes* held honored places leading off the processions, only to quietly disappear the other 364 days of the year, lest they become politically inconvenient. It was the homo equivalent of the mythical Scottish village *Brigadoon*, which appeared only at very specific times, and then only for the briefest of interludes, before vanishing entirely from sight once again.

With the desexualization and de-gendering of the Homosexual complete, for political purposes, gay people were no longer "*just like* straight people"—gay people *were* straight people. Author Lisa Duggan termed the emergence of this new hetero-gay, anchored in neoliberal consumption and domesticity, as "homonormativity."[58,59] As Susan Stryker notes, gay rights accomplished this through promoting a tacit agreement between itself and heterosexual culture about what a Man and a Woman were, an agreement which would have been largely unavailable had it continued to foreground trans people and genderqueer gays, lesbians, and bisexuals.[60] In addition, eliding sex enabled the emerging homonormative gay movement to avoid dealing with the gender implications of two grown men having anal or oral sexual intercourse, even though such acts are the very definition of queerness and gender deviance.[61]

Strangely enough, all this occurred even as mainstream visibility and acceptance of the figure of the Drag Queen expanded exponentially through shows like RuPaul's *Drag Race*, movies like *Paris Is Burning*, and the proliferation in local schools of Drag Queen Story Hours. But drag could be written off as entertainment, a staged performance, one that came to an end when the glitter came off. It was not what the gay men *were*.

The fact that gay discourse no longer spoke the language of gender or sexuality fed an immense overhang between the public's vision of the new homonormative gay and of the reality that sexuality and gender deviance are still very integral to homosexuality. And since 2019, white Christian nationalists have been eagerly and vilely leveraging this void of knowledge with their usual vile canards about gays being "groomers" who are "sexualizing" children.

"The Only Thing That Makes You Interesting Is Me"

As a quick test of just how successfully sexuality has been actually removed as a site—let alone a *privileged site*—of queer inquiry, I turned to Google Scholar. I realize this is a rough-edged tool at best, and has become even rougher as Google has refined its search results based on prior searches as well as Google's own interests, author prominence, journal venue, cites by other articles, and so on—so while it's much less personalized than Google Search, it's still far from a data-neutral reflection of what's out there. However, I don't think it qualifies as useless either, if the results are taken with a large grain of salt.

My searches for the word "queering" in the title peer-reviewed articles, showing that using "queer" as an adjective is not just one aspect of queer theory, but has morphed into its own academic subspecialty. The first two Google pages alone list *queering* history, ethics, plays, texts, K-pop, the Renaissance, Asia, ecology, nonhumans, historical archives, and so on and so forth.

Then I turned to "queering sex," which returned only fifteen articles, "queering sexuality" just seven, and "queering desire" a paltry five. Consider the following breakdown of my searchers of the titles of four of the better-known "legacy" queer studies journals which have the largest number of published articles:

	Journal of Homosexuality	Journal of Lesbian Studies	Gay & Lesbian Studies	GLQ
Butch	1	16	4	2
Feminine/effeminate/sissy	4	1	1	1
Bottoms*	0	1	1	1
Gender and gay men	4	0	2	2
Fag	5	2	1	1
Drag	+++	6	4	2
Trans/transgender	+++	+++	+++	+++

*titles about gay or male, lesbian, or women (but not trans)

+++ too many titles to count

As I mentioned, Google Scholar is not the final word. And the field is much, much broader than just these four. Scholars have written about sex and queerness without using these search terms, and newer journals would likely return more hits than are displayed here.[62] In addition, there are many outstanding individual exceptions such as Leo Bersani's landmark essay "Is the Rectum a Grave," and Cathy Cohen's "Punks, Bulldaggers, and Welfare Queens."[63]

Bearing all those caveats in mind, this example does provide at least some very rough indication of just how just how successfully both deviant gender and deviant sex have been absent from the mainstream of academic thought.

The familiar figures of fairies and sissies, who haunted narratives of gayness's past, disreputable erotic acts like anal and oral "sodomy," and even the anarchic and scandalous desire for hot and anonymous sex often historically (if sometimes wrongly) associated with the Homosexual—all of this has moved to the margins of critical interest as queer pedagogic consciousness has largely turned its attention elsewhere.

Even queer theory's many books and articles on drag— as performance, as parody, as art form, as cultural display, as resistance—seldom interrogate it as means for gay men to display male femininity in a publicly acceptable manner, nor any feelings of eroticism or sexuality that they might attach to the hyperfeminine gender expressions they are performing. Instead, all gender deviance is reflected onto other, more marginal bodies and subaltern identities.

Or as Stryker puts it:

> "[T]"ransgender increasingly functions as the site in which to contain all gender trouble, thereby helping secure both homosexuality and heterosexuality as stable and normative categories of personhood. . . . It is the same developmental logic that transformed an antiassimilationist "queer" politics into a more

palatable LGBT civil rights movement, with T reduced to merely another (easily detached) genre of sexual identity.[64]

I believe that this dynamic has occurred at least in part because transgender may ultimately prove more undigestible to the cishet binary than was gayness. For instance, I think it's a different kind of epistemologic *stretch* to accommodate the idea of gay marriage than it is (for example) of nonbinary genders, women's penises, and pregnant men—all of which force us to rethink the body and sexes in very fundamental ways. In any case today, as scholars from David Eng to (more recently) Cáel Keegan have noted, the queerest thing left about queer theory *is* transgender.[65,66] Or, as Henry Rubin put it all the way back in 1998, trans is *queer chic*.[67]

All this is reminiscent of the gender-bending hit show *Killing Eve*, in which the psychopathic but ravishing international female assassin Villanelle reminds the drab-but-dogged MI6 investigator Eve Pollastri pursuing her across three continents through a combustible mixture of stubbornness and sublimated sexual fixation: "Don't forget: the only thing that makes you interesting is me."

A Geography of the Absent

Even as it was erased from public discourse, "deviant" sexual and gendered pleasures such BD/SM, fisting, rimming, snowballing, water sports, and so on were still common in the gay community. There were still entire subcultures devoted to drag, fairies, bears, latex, tea-rooms, rough trade, and so on. While certainly not all gay men engaged in these, there was plenty that remained "deviant" about gay male sexualities and genders (as with straight and bisexual ones). But it was no longer centered in queer theory or study, much less discussed in polite society.[68]

Straight people had long reduced gay people to their sexuality. Now this key facet of gayness vanished forever from queer theory. Not because the subject was theoretically exhausted—quite the contrary— but because queer theory, like gay rights, preferred to give them as little formal acknowledgment as possible. The modern hetero-gay rights movement and queer academia created an entire *geography of the absent*—people who weren't mentioned, acts and desires that weren't discussed, nonnormative genders one didn't acknowledge.

For these, queer theory was forced to turn to the Transsexual, the Intersex, and the Transgender—including the Drag Queen—for figures it could mobilize in its quest to "problematize" heteronormativity.[69]

Queer academics studiously ignored the sexual and gender deviance of the sodomite and the fairy in favor of focusing exclusively on the supposed sexual or gender deviance of these small minorities within minorities who remained unassimilable within the new homonormativity which had just consumed the Homosexual. Thus, queer theory books like *Gender Trouble* often go on at great length about transsexual and transgender people, or the intersex/DSD, but of genderqueer gays and lesbians they remain entirely silent. Even books devoted to the Homosexual like Eve Kosofsky Sedgwick's *Epistemology of the Closet* have little to say about genderqueerness among gays, lesbians, or bisexuals or anything about their erotic practices.[70,71]

Henceforth, to speak to a queer theorist or a gay advocate about gender was to inevitably be answered with something about a transsexual or a transgender person, which was the only remaining register in which such things could still be spoken. As anthropologist David Valentine noted in "We're Not about Gender" with obvious understatement, today "gender has ceased to be a site for the discussion of gay and lesbian lives."[72]

Undoing Exclusion

Predictably, the exclusion of genderqueerness from homosexuality gave rise to a reverse discourse. The queerness which had once attached itself to the Homosexual now took up theoretical and political residence in Transgender.

Before the emergence of nonbinary, genderfluid, and other subaltern identities, "Transgender" meant just transsexuals and crossdressers. The latter, who were mostly male and overwhelming hetero, were ignored by queer theory (more on this later), although they constituted outstanding examples of subverting masculinity in ways that were much more profound than the Drag Queen.

As the homonormativity of gay discourse disconnected itself from gender, trans people who had spent years in gay politics, bars, communities, and rights found themselves outside their own movement looking in. Gay discourse increasingly understood itself as devoted solely to sexual orientation and Transgender as a separate cause. It was suddenly required to explain itself, to document a history within the queer community going back decades of which everyone was well aware, but which—because it was now politically inconvenient—had suddenly become obscure.

Just as cisgender medico-psychiatric power demanded that Transgender subject produce a justificatory narrative for gender-affirming care, so the new hetero-gay movement demanded that the Transgender subject produce a justificatory case for inclusion within a political movement which the rebellions by low-income, Black, and Latinx transgender people had just ignited at San Francisco's Compton's Cafeteria Riot and NYC's Stonewall Riots.

So the transgender movement made its case. And then, for over a decade, the new hetero-gay movement simply rejected it.

Butches, who had been derided as *he-she's* and gay men who had endured boyhood taunting for being *sissies* and *fairies* and who had had marched in parades with trans people, fought cops with trans people, and had done ACT-UP die-ins with trans people, suddenly insisted that Gender Identity Is Different from Sexual Orientation, and required its own separate movement.

A bitter two-decade struggle erupted over this new and fictitious division, as the white, hetero-gay movement agonized endlessly whether it should reintegrate within its political ranks the very people it had just excluded for its own political ends, and what was actually a battle to *undo trans-exclusion* was cast—without irony—as one over *becoming trans-inclusive*.

It was as if transgender people were some long-lost relative, showing up unannounced just as the will was to be read, posing inconvenient questions about the coming family inheritance. And when at last Transgender was reintegrated back into the gay movement it had helped launched and from which it had been expunged, this was celebrated as a great moral victory. T was affixed to the ass-end of LGB, where it remains today.[73] But by then, Elvis had definitely left the building.

"A Very Neat System": De-Gendering Gayness and De-Sexing Transness

Anthropologist David Valentine has pointed out in a series of passionately argued papers and a full-length book that the deployment of simplistic binaries like gender/sex and gay/trans don't always map onto nonnormative genders and sexualities that are non-Western, of color, and/or economically marginalized.[74]

As he puts it, "It is this unmarked sense of gay that I will examine in this chapter, and it is this meaning I employ when I invoke 'gay.' At the same time, I will show how (desexualized) category of 'transgender' has filled the empty space left by such a de-gendering."[75]

Among Valentine's starting points for his argument are Nora—a Latinx trans counselor—and Angel, a Black trans member of Nora's support group.[76] Angel variously refers to herself as *gay*, a *woman with a penis*, a *transsexual*, and a *homosexual man with breasts*.

As a trans-identified woman, Nora repeatedly prods Angel to disambiguate her multiple and overlapping these identities, to recognize and announce that she is actually and only a *transgender woman*—specifically a *transsexual woman*.

But Angel resists this move, locating herself and moving freely among these subject positions, depending upon what is being discussed: her gender identity, her social existence, her sex life, and so on.

At one point in the back-and-forth that ensues, Angel metaphorically throws up her hands, declaring: "When it comes down to sex, I don't think . . . it's two men going to bed with each other, a man and a woman going to bed with it or pre-op or nothing like that. I just think it's just two people having sex, making love to each other." As Valentine correctly notes, Angel is proposing a fluidity to sexual identity that neatly encapsulates a nonidentitarian politics of sexual desire.

He picks up the same theme in talks with Fiona, whom we might consider another trans woman of color, but who like Angel also refuses to simplify her identity within conventional categories, identifying as a "fem queen" while explaining at the same time that, "I've been gay all my life and a woman all my life."[77]

Trans studies often observes that transgender is an identity complicated by factors like race and class. But it seldom extends that observation to note how this is implicated in many of those it implicitly identifies as being *transgender* and those who also still self-identify as *gay*. (A failing I will have sometimes replicated here myself.)

Valentine notes that in queer and trans academia, gay and trans "identities are seen to flow from distinct kinds of ontological sources—transgender identity from 'gender,' and homosexual identity from 'sexuality' [in a] very neat system which accounts both for erotic desire and gender identification." Or once again, as Rubin put it, the "basis of two distinct arenas of social practice."

Yet, for Fiona and Angel illustrate, "there are other ways of organizing the experiences of nonnormative genders and sexualities" than gay/trans, ways in which sexual orientation and gender identity are not separate and distinct arenas, but rather radically contingent upon one another.

In the ball culture of Valentine's anthropological work, *everyone* doing their various genders is considered "gay"—butch queens, fem queens, transwomen, butch lesbians, gay men—because *gay* is understood in its original sense, as "indexing any gendered or sexual difference that marks you off from heteronormativity. . . . [M] asculine-identified homosexual men and feminine-identified women are as much a part of the category 'gay' in this context as are femme queens and butches."

That is, gay is still used in all its pre-homonormative and pre-commodification breadth, when the deviance of same-sex sexuality and the gender deviance were understood as intertwined, overlapping, and often co-occurring in the same individuals. Until the recent advent of homonormative discourse, gay sexual desire itself was always widely understood as inherently gender nonconforming: "Two men kissing or engaging in anal sex could as easily be understood as gendered acts as they could sexual acts."[78] In conventional terms, what could be more queering of traditional masculinity than a man assuming the receptive or "feminine" position during intercourse?

Angel and Fiona's insistence on claiming all their identities as a gay men with breasts, transsexual women with penises, fem queens, trans, and simply as *gay* challenges and disrupts the "very neat system" which queer and trans studies have both adopted in order to theorize an orderly world that does not and never did exist.

As Valentine explains, we could respond that Fiona, "Rita or Jade or Miss Angel are laboring under 'false consciousness' because they are unable to distinguish their 'gendered' and 'sexual' identities?" But saying so would "assert a modernist telos wherein the recognition of gendered and sexual identification as separate is more accurate, more true, more valid. Thus, the Meat Market fem queens like Rita become almost figures of premodernity, people who have not been 'educated,' who adhere to the 'mistaken' belief that homosexual identification involves cross-gender identification."[79]

Flattening Identities

Subjectivities like Angel's and Fiona's "have fallen out of a categorical system where their own understandings of self can be understood." Their identities, gendered embodiment, and phenomenological experience of their own erotic activities is erased, rendered unrepresentable and unintelligible within the very queer/trans field which emerged to represent and valorize them but which—because it has pursued this goal by imposing discrete categories of sexuality and gender—is unable to account for them.

Even as trans studies has made great strides in become more intersectional in its engagement with factors like race, class, culture, incarceration, and HIV status, bodies like Angel's and Fiona's—which exist at complex intersections of gender with poverty, racism, and culture—still "fall out of this categorical system where their own understandings of self" are no longer recognized.

Trans scholarship has increasingly called out this kind of erasure or "flattening" of identities when Western, Eurocentric understandings of "trans" are imposed on diverse non-white populations such as the Muxe of Mexico, two-spirit of the American West, hijra of India, and so on.[80] But trans studies also unintentionally inflicts a very similar epistemic violence its marginalized identities right here in America through the very terms of its own epistemic emergence.

As more identities emerged that are even more confounding to the binary—such as genderqueer, genderfluid, agender, and nonbinary— it is unclear how trans studies will apply the "very neat system" to them as well. Recently, I was interviewing trans/nonbinary people about their sexuality and using my standard questionnaire, I asked an interviewee their sexual orientation. They gave me a long pause, and then said, "Well, there's never a good answer to that when you're nonbinary." Duhhh.

Is a nonbinary person always having heterosexual sex except when they are with another nonbinary? And the same for a couple who are genderqueer, even though one of them might be transmasculine and the other transfeminine? Is a genderfluid person having homosexual sex only when they are with another person whose is also genderfluid, or only when their gender identities aligns at that moment—such as when one is femme-identified and the other is currently feme-identified?

Whatever the answer to questions like these, it seems hard to reestablish any kind of bright-line distinction between sexuality and gender once we step completely off the binary.

Perhaps my questions seem frivolous. But 60 percent of trans-identified people in Gen Z—currently, the world's largest generation—do *not* identify within simple binary categories of "trans boy" versus "trans girl." As they increasingly come of age and embrace a bewildering multiplicity of identities, such questions may become more pressing for trans scholarship to address.[81]

Stay in Your Own Yard

It is tempting to suggest that queer and trans studies have forgotten that the distinction between the sexual and gender are, like the identities and subjectivities, to some degree the result of specific needs, times, and arrangements of power. As Valentine puts it in his book, *Imagining Transgender*, "In asserting the truth of the distinction between gender and sexuality—rather than recognizing that it is simply one way of carving up how we know about ourselves and others—contemporary critical social theory engages all those aspects of modernity that in other guises it critiques: a master narrative, unfolding within a historical teleology, characterized by progress and a coming-to-truth."[82]

In other words, the epistemic structures of trans theory and its emergence as a field are disrupted by such *unruly bodies* like Angel's and Fiona's in much the same way that queer theory used the *unruly* transsexual and intersex/DSD bodies to disrupt the epistemic structures of heteronormativity.

To absorb such subjects under the transgender umbrella, we must first simplify them in ways that render them unrecognizable to themselves. For there is no category within transgender which is defined, or even co-defined, by its sexuality.

Just as Valentine has noted that gender is not a site for a discussion of gay and lesbian lives, so sexuality is not a site for discussion of transgender lives.[83] "[T]he varied experiences of cross-gender expressions, practices, and identities gathered under this term [transgender] present a challenge to a set of theoretical relations upon which" queer and trans scholarship are based[84]—that is, the theoretical separation of sexuality and gender.

This is a polite, academic way of saying the emperor has no clothes.

Perhaps not unexpectedly, Valentine's arguments, despite being widely cited in queer papers, tend to be honored by "citation without consideration." The fact that neither queer nor trans theorists have taken them more seriously is a sign of field's reluctance to interrogate the conditions and assumptions of its own emergence.[85]

No doubt there are gays who are entirely gender-normative, and trans people who are entirely sexually normative. But the academic conceit of this false separation does justice to neither the gay nor the transgender lives to which this is applied. "[L]eather men who camp it up, 'butches vogueing butch queen vogueing fem,' nellie men who body build, dykes in leather who are femmes, transqueers, genderfuckers, femme bois, radical fairies, queers, drag queens for a day, men, women, and others in multiple-partner families, fem queens who enjoy penetrative anal sex, butch bears who wear lingerie, and a vast range of other expressions of self and desire" are all subjects that provide ample opportunity to interrogate gender deviance across gay, lesbian, and bi sexual practice. But the figure of the Transsexual has always been catnip to queer theorists, even when other equally "insubordinate" identities are flourishing in their own backyard.[86] (Interestingly, trans studies has also remained largely disinterested in interrogating the genders and gender identities of such subjects, simply because they are not trans.)

Beginning to engage with what trans

people say about what they desire, who they desire, and how they act upon those desires can highlight for us the political nature of desire, and the ways such yearnings are shaped by the identity categories through which they are forced to speak. . . . It would enable us to look more closely at the seemingly neutral categories of "gender" and "sexuality," and complicate the relationship between them [rather than] simply assuming that desire is self-evidently explained by them.[87]

For Valentine, this interrogating and complicating the erotic lives of trans people would open up an important series of questions that lie at the heart of trans studies but are so far unaddressed, among them:

- How is the sexual constituted when it is confined solely to the object and direction of desire?

- What are the historical conditions for the emergence of the sex/gender—gay/trans distinction?

- In what ways might the sex/gender division be a contingent, rather than natural, distinction?

- What other configurations of sex/gender are possible?

- What are the power dynamics between those subcultures that valorize this distinction and those that continue to refute it? What might this arrangement say about the distinction itself?

- In what ways does the sex/gender binary depend on or require binary heteronormative subjects for its intelligibility?

So I return to my earlier question: Can trans studies hope to understand gender without also understanding (trans) sexuality?

New Under the Sun

Perhaps queer theorists have so little to say about queer sexualities and genders because they believe there is nothing new to say about them. But there is a *lot* new to say about transgender sexualities and genders.

Because many of us inhabit bodies and experience pleasures that have never existed. To be perhaps too blunt, I have intercourse with a vagina constructed from a skin graft off my butt, and a clitoris constructed from the glans of what used to be my penis. I have friends who have intercourse with vaginas constructed from their inverted penises or from their colons. Now when in the 300,000 years since *Homo sapiens* emerged from the African savannahs have bodies and experiences quite like these ever existed?[88,89]

Part of what Laura Horak has called *genital time* is the sense that in pursuit and realization of surgery, a linear chronology opens up "beginning with a moment of rupture and pointing . . . toward a utopian future" in which the promise of the *right body* is finally realized.[90]

When I first had surgery, it was like that, and I expected to wake up with new vagina feeling . . . well, completely vaginal. But I awoke in the Recovery Room and was instantly, massively disappointed. While I don't know what a factory-installed vagina feels like, I *do* know what a penis feels like, and nothing felt all that different.

This was not what I expected at all. Even weirder, I could actually feel the same nerve endings in my groin and visualize where they used to live on the geography of my now-absent penis. While mildly interesting at first, it was also deeply disorienting and I quickly stopped doing it.

But such experiences raise interesting questions about how homologous the female and male *phallus* really are and whether perhaps genital sensations between male and female bodies are less different than we might expect and are not only mediated by actual differences in nerve endings but by the way we embody and eroticize their configuration.

When it comes to physically rearranging genitals—whether because of sex reassignment, injury, or malformation—perhaps neuroplasticity in the unconscious postoperative bodily schema shifts according to rhythms and logic we have yet to comprehend, and our bodies adjust via unanticipated pathways, across unexpected thresholds, and in specific stages we have yet to discover.

Certainly, it is a strange process of integrating new organs (which in my case were still undergoing minor follow-on operations and thus a work-in-progress) into one's sense of embodiment, and thence into pleasure, and finally into intimacy. It was like flying a new plane while still building it.

Today when I have vaginal sex, in my mind it certainly *feels* like something I identify *as* vaginal sex. I have no sense of my prior penis or my butt, and it's certainly completely different from anal sex. But how could I know, since I've never had a vagina before? Indeed, there's a likelihood that even those with factory-equipped vaginas don't all feel the same thing, or that there *is* any prototypical essentialized experience that feels like "vaginal sex." (For an example of this conundrum, see poet Jody Rose's quote below.)

I remain stumped for any good phenomenological or theoretical explanation for how I can experience a distinct and distinctly pleasurable form of arousal, pleasure, and climax from an organ my body has never had before. How can clitoral pleasure *feel* like something I can identify *as* clitoral pleasure, when it comes from nerve endings that originated in a different organ in a different configuration? How can stimulating such organs be not only pleasurable erotica and psychologically satisfying in a way that the former configuration was so utterly not?

After all, it was not that I didn't find penile sex and orgasm physically pleasurable; just that it was erotically uninteresting, often repellant, and detached from arousal. But then how is it that having a vagina radically revamps this experience of erotic embodiment? How does this alchemy occur, and what does it mean for our understanding of the body, its phenomenology, and its erotic capacity—not just for the trans body but for the human body itself?

There were a lot of unexpected and unpleasant psychological quirks in my new embodiment as well. When I was in a deep sleep and had to urinate (which, as I've gotten older is only about as often as I breath), my brain apparently needed to generate a rationale for my not relieving my bladder.

So in my dreams it would often situate me in a Women's Room where I was unable to relieve myself because the other women were confronting me about having a penis. Needless to say, this was extremely unpleasant to wake up to, over and over again. And of course, since it was a dream, I was totally helpless to do anything about it until, after years, it finally stopped. (A good reason to be kind to your unconscious.)

I was reminded of this while reading "One Man's Junk" in *Hung Jury*, in which the writer Declan writes: "I'd have nightmares about strangers angrily grabbing my crotch and shouting at me that I had no penis." It makes me wonder if the specter of cishostility is a common trauma that haunts many transsexuals who have undergone genital surgeries.[91] Perhaps many of us internalize transphobia in deeper and more profound ways than we realize.

Similarly, whenever I had sex in my dreams (which, unfortunately, was *much* less frequently than my having to pee), I would still often have a penis. Naturally, this dream was also either distressing or simply weird. But eventually, I would wake up groggy from a dream about sex and realize, "Oh, I had a *vagina* for that one"—accompanied by a vague sense of accomplishment and satisfaction.

Prosser has argued about trans men that postsurgical embodiment works as well as it does because they already have "psychic penises."[92]

But what could this mean? Are there two and only two archetypal psychic genitalia that all of us possess? Or are other configurations possible? Do any of us, for example, have "psychic intersex genitals?" I recently interviewed a Salmacian woman who had both a natal penis and a surgically created vagina; what kind of Prosser-type organ might have been in her head? Are all psychic penises and vaginas essentialized and thus the same, or are they socially contingent? Or do they vary by race, class, and other factors? Why might the experiences of the re/de/constructed transsexual body tell us about those of cisgender bodies, particularly those re/de/constructed in ways like ours because of injury or malformation?

We can't yet answer such questions, because—although they may be integral to the transsexual experience *qua transsexual*—we have not attempted any critical interrogation of them. Thus, we have no theoretical tools to grapple with them. And no, I don't think continuing to recycle Husserl and Merleau-Ponty is going to get us there. We are going to have to create new tools from scratch, and, to my mind, it is critical work that transgender people are uniquely situated to do.

A Language of Gender Neologisms

And not just theoretical tools but also new language and terminology. As nonbinary theorist Hari Ziyad notes, "[E]very day there is a new term to describe the countless different ways that people experience (or don't experience) gender. . . . We are operating within a language that does not make room for us. . . . [W]e are always 'scouring for tools in an empty shed.'"[93]

If the linguistic shed *is* empty, trans people themselves have been remarkably creative at resisting cislogocentric discourse in at least two ways. First, we reframe and transform words and names, cutting them to a better fit.

As theorist H. Howitt explains in their magisterial paper, "How We Fuck":

The adoption or rejection of discursive practices is a component of all trans sex assemblages. [We] engage in a language practice, or have others engage in language practices to address the difficulty of talking about our bodies, what we like to have done to them, and what we want to do with them . . . renaming or reframing certain body parts and sex acts to achieve a greater sense of gendered congruence.[94]

As they note, this semiotic practice has important material effects on arousal and sensation, decreasing dysphoria while increasing the ability to desire sex, experience pleasure, even to orgasm.

And second, we are generating an enormous and growing dialect of trans-centric neologisms, appropriations, and portmanteaus. Here are some of the Anglophone ones for genitalia and sexual orientation/ desire:

Bigenitals, bonus hole, boycunt, dic-clit/diclit/dikclet, front endosex, hole, girldick, mancunt,mangina, manhole, minicock, Nullo, and *trannycock.Biromantic, demisexual, pansexual, greysexual, protogay, skoliosexual/scoliosexual, transfan,transfag, transphile/transphilia,* and *tryke.*There is also an expanding vocabulary to describe gendered identities, including the following:

Agemder, androgyne, aporagender, bigender, boi/boi-girl, biogirl/ bioguy, butch-queen, cisfeminine/cismasculine, demigirl/demiboy, demisexual, egg, enby, fae, femme queen, gender affirming, gender confirming, gender hybrid, gender nonconforming, genderfluid, genderless, genderfuck, genderqueer, gender smoothie, gender-variant, graygender, grrl, intergender, ladyboi, maverique, MOGAI-IMOGA (marginalized orientations gender alignments & intersex), multigender, muxe, neutrois, nonbinary, nondysphoric/ pro-nondysphoric, nontransgender, nontranssexual, novigender, onigender, pangender, polygender, poxogender, prototransgender, Salmacian, skoliosexual/ scoliosexual,theyby, third gender, translatina, trannie/tranny, transgender, trans, trans*, transfeminine/

transmasculine, transgenderist, trigender, transing, Two-Spirit, xenogender.

Trans-centric language generation has also become an important source of trans resistance through humor. Florence Ashley lists the following for surgery, including the following:

> *Ballbusting, chop chop, cuntsmithing, Free Willy, genital origami, genital switcharoo surgery, his-terectomy, junk removal, late-term circumcision, meat delete, snatch switch, teetus deletus,* and *teet yeet.*[95]

Some of these are others used only in specific trans subcultures, other are more likely protologisms: newly coined words that may go on to secure wider use or just disappear. In fact, some here are older now and used very rarely, if at all. For instance, it is hard to imagine the plethora of newly minted microlabels and neopronouns popular in online communities and/or, among those of us who are neurodivergent, still being around in a few years.

In some cases, trans people are attempting to recenter trans bodies by recasting the meanings of body parts and resisting cisnormative meanings for them. Consider the following excerpt from transmasculine writer/poet Jody Rose:

> I'm finally admitting that I don't mind having a vagina. Why does it matter if I feel pleasure there? It doesn't have to be defined as "female" pleasure; pleasure is pleasure, and I don't need to label or define my pleasure based on gender. . . . I have a masculine, male vagina with an enlarged two-inch clit that gets think and hard and can get sucked—that can go inside a woman. . . . I can have sex with

enlarged clit/dick, and when I do it, my vagina gets wet. . . . My vagina is masculine. It's aggressive and powerful. It takes charge and control, and it dominates. . . . I'm proud of my vagina. And why does the word "vagina" have to be associated with only women, anyway?[96]

In each sentence, one can hear Rose struggling manfully to re-signify his body and to resist the signification imposed on it by the semiotics available to describe it. In the last sentence, he even metaphorically throws up his hands in frustration, asking, *why does this word have to mean something which obliterates what I want to say in the very act of saying it?*

Similarly, as Bellwether wrote in "Fucking Trans Women":

[A]lmost all sexual discourse on penises is on erect penises, hard penises, engorged penises. . . . Because the operating assumption in our culture is that only hard penises can have sex, that soft penises can't have sex and aren't sexy. . . . [A] soft penis is not a "Do Not Disturb" sign.

Soft penises are one of the most neglected subjects in studies of sexuality. . . . I've yet to find a single article, essay, story, or description of a sexy soft penis. . . . They're the punch line of a joke with no setup, no content, only mute assumptions and expectations that all cocks are rock-hard. If not, they're assumed to be useless or pathetic or both. . . . I'm spent hours looking for something written on the topic of pleasuring soft penises, and I found nothing [except] ways to make them erect.[97,98]

Bellwether even promoted a novel way to have penetrative sex with a natal male body: penetrating the inguinal canals, those small cavities from which testes descend, an act she called "muffing."[99,100]

Lacan and the critical theorists used the term *phallogocentrism* to refer to the privileging of a masculine-signifying economy over all alternatives (phallus = masculine, logos = word). I would call systems of meaning founded on and are organized around the binary cishetero signifying economy as *cislogocentrism*.

And Rose's and Bellwether's frustration here points to the problem of cislogocentric forms of knowledge, which not only render aspects of abjected experience unthinkable, but which are designed and intended to do so.

Fricker notes, *contra* Foucault and Bulter, that there are "direct and indirect psychological harms of being unable to make one's experiences intelligible to others, and of the associated quality-of-life costs of being unable to articulate and address one's needs" because one is denied the language resources to make sense of one's self, which she calls *hermeneutic injustice*.[101]

Yet, as Zimman notes in "Transgender Language Reform," despite widespread recognition of the challenges normative gendered language poses for trans people and of the centrality of language to identify formation and self-recognition, this extensive and unique subaltern lexicon has received surprisingly little attention from scholars of language and gender or from trans academics. This may in part be due to the low social and scholarly value given to the linguistic practices of abjected groups as a "serious" topic for study.[102]

If the title of Judith Butler's second book was "Bodies That Matter," the subtitle of Fricker's first might have been "Voices That Matter." While Butler's postmodernism foregrounded the marginalization of abjected bodies and their discursive construction, Fricker's hermeneutics placed that marginalization within an explicit, ethical framework, showing how discursive representation was a crucial component in providing justice to abjected subjects.

The Power of Meaning

Both trans scholarship and transgender rights promote the proposition that trans people have the right to define themselves and their bodies, or what Talia Mae Bettcher has termed First Person Authority.[103] But the invention and deployment of new terms and meanings for trans bodies, genitalia, and desires raise interesting questions about the limits of FPA that mostly go unaddressed.

This is neatly summarized in one ironic video by the Instagram influencer, kelz koch, in which the following dialog develops between a father as he drives his daughter. Even though they use the same words, the discursive systems within which they interpret them are completely at odds and so not really on speaking terms with one another. [*Edited for length—Ed.*]

Daughter: . . . Oh, and Mary Margaret showed me her penis.
[Car brakes a sudden squealing halt.]
Father : Some boy showed you his penis?
D: What? No, not a boy Daddy. Gross! Mary Margaret. She's a girl.
F: Girls don't have penises, Winnie.
D: Mary Margaret does. Penises are weird.
F: Can we stop saying *penis* please? Where did this happen, anyway?
D: In the bathroom.

F: Well, why are they letting boys in the girls bathroom?

D: Why do you keep misgendering Mary Margaret?

F: Misgendering? What are you talking about?

D: It's very transphobic of you.

F: How do you know the word 'transphobic'?

D: I'm eight years old!

F: Exactly! You're eight years old!

D: Okay, boomer.[104]

Does FPA extend equally to all parts of the transfeminine body: Pre-op, non-op, post-op? Are a nonoperative girldick, a postoperative neo-clit, and a factory-installed clit all clitorises in the same way and all gendered in the same way if their owners pronounce them so? The same could be asked of the mancunt, the metoidioplasty dick, and phalloplasty dick and the factory-installed dick.

Does and should FPA authority extend past gender identity to the realm of how we want our bodies' physical properties and their erotic esthetics understood ? As Bellwether writes in "Fucking Trans Women," "Trans women's bodies are soft . . . because we say they are. . . . My body is a woman's body and part of it is my penis. . . . I don't think anyone has every complimented me on how sexy my penis looks when it's soft, but whatever: it's totally sexy."[105]

Are there any limits to FPA? If there are, who is authorized to make that decision and by whom?

And if there are not—and I don't think there are or should be—trans theory needs to be laying the intellectual foundation for what this actually means when it's taken to its logical conclusions beyond assertions, that is, "Trans woman are women, period." I suspect we are going to have to do a lot more theoretical, political, and polemical work to move than to say, "Girldicks are female organs, period," and also "Frontholes are male organs, period." Truly overturning cislogocentrism means going beyond the right to claim our position as women or men (or nonbinary) within the prevailing cishet discourse or coining new words: it will mean the tools and theory that can challenge its entire underlying epistemic structure.

Of Crossdressing Elephants

I said earlier that "transgender" used to mean mostly just transsexuals and of course crossdressers, who were long its most visible members. Yet when queer *and* trans theorists write Transgender, they refer only to transsexuals. Both seldom engage with nonbinary, genderqueer, agender, and genderfluid trans people, and both have (almost) entirely ignored the figure of the Crossdresser.

There may be hundreds of thousands of transsexuals in the United States—estimates vary between 1:500 and 1:2,000. But there is at least an order of magnitude more crossdressers—easily in the millions (again, estimate run between 1:15 or 1:20, with maybe 1:33 doing dressing regularly).[106,107,108] Taking the latter number yields about four million regular crossdressers, with six million or more having crossdressed at least once.

From this perspective, I'm not sure what to make of the usually reliable Williams Institute's widely quoted estimate of 1.6 million transgender-identified adults.[109] Except to assume that they are completely ignoring crossdressers as well, or using a very narrow technical definition of "transgender" that does not count those who identity as nonbinary, genderqueer, or gender fluid.

But when it comes to things transgender, straight male crossdressers are definitely the elephant in the room. This is an enormous population of gender nonconforming individuals hiding in plain sight that attracts little scholarly attention or critical theorizing, and has been barely studied. In a sign of academia's continuing indifference, one or the more widely cited prevalence studies is from 1997—over a quarter century old.[110,111]

Why the lack of theoretic and critical interest?

Certainly one factor is that while the figure of the Drag Queen is often associated with edginess, campy humor, glitz, and fashion-forwardness, the figure of the crossdresser is more often associated with being older, heterosexual, and fashion-backward. In other words, less Ru Paul in the latest Dior *haute couture* and more your aunt in Evan-Picone from Macy's Womenswear section. (Don't laugh—I wore this when I first transitioned.)

If the Drag Queen's campy parody fashion send-ups of gender and femininity and the postoperative Transsexual's bodily "subversion" of gender norms are seen as the kind of "insubordinacy" that queer theorists find irresistible, the Crossdresser offers neither the glamour, the fashion, the irony nor anything so physically radical as genital alterations: nothing but the embrace of primary male femininity.

If this weren't enough to render him aesthetically and intellectually uninteresting to queer and trans theorists, there's also the bigger problem of his sexuality.

Although the idea that transsexual (women) were just auto-fetishists was always a vile academic canard, a substantial percentage of men actually pursue crossdressing because of its erotic appeal: either the clothing themselves or the experience of dressing in them (or both) is sexually arousing.

The idea of men *getting off* on clothing has proven strangely uncomfortable territory for queer and trans scholars.[112] Yet I've followed the International Mr. Leather contest, and I'm pretty sure those guys aren't fitting themselves in head-to-toe leather and studs toe because it makes them feel asexual, or because it turns potential sex partners off. Similarly, Victoria's Secret didn't build a multibillion-dollar business based on the fact that its millions of women feel utterly neutered when wearing its popular split crotch panties, push-up bras, and Baby Doll nighties.

As for the "cross" part of crossdressing, men can hardly be blamed for that. Unlike the vast majority of higher species, in which sexual displays and erotic plumage are province of the male, among *Homo sapiens* only the female performs them. Legs, arms, and chests are exposed; color is applied, which makes the mouths appear puffy, pouty, and engorged; ink around the eyes and on the lashes make them look wide with interest; powder flushes the cheeks with artificial arousal; and high heels raise and tighten the buttocks to present them as if for mating—not all that dissimilar from the sexual swelling of the same area that occurs among many female primates to signal fertility.[113]

So many of the main ways for the human male to express public sexuality, or experience feeling lascivious and "slutty" as a sex object, is by utilizing gender expressions and body modifications associated with and socially restricted to the human female.

But besides his straightness, I think what really makes the Crossdresser uncomfortable for trans theory is that he sexualizes *gender*. We are taught to always say that we want to dress in certain clothes or change certain body parts because it expresses our inner *gender identity*, because it is *who we are*. It contradicts the foundational discourse of trans studies and of transgender rights to say that one wants to wear women's clothes or live *en femme* because it gets you hot or makes you feel kind of slutty. It delegitimates the entire justificatory discourse patiently built up over decades around transition, hormones, and surgery. And it undercuts or at least complicates the claims of transgender as a protected class under civil rights law.

The fact that the figure of the Crossdresser is at once so well-known, so universally disdained by heteronormative culture, and also so ignored by most of queer and trans academia should alert trans scholars that something profound is going on here worthy of real attention. Not to mention—as theorist Ciara Cremin notes about patriarchy—"[T]he path to liberation passes through the feminine . . . [because] femininity is the specter that haunts the psyche."[114,115]

The figure of a cishetero man who owns his own primary femininity for both its gender and its sexuality complicates heteronormativity and cisnormativity in ways that are unavailable to the Drag Queen and the Transsexual. But a queer theory so focused on irony, parody, and insubordination, on the one hand, and a trans studies so focused on the seriousness of valorizing gender identities, on the other, both remain unable to appreciate how radical a straight man embracing male feminine sexuality is.

Not that we're engaged in any kind contest here, but it has always seemed to me like crossdressing is in many ways the more radical, subversive, and despised act.

First, there may be thousands of US transgender people who are out—including many public figures—but while they identify variously as transsexual, nonbinary, genderqueer and so on, to my knowledge there are *none* who are out who identify publicly as male crossdressers. This shows how difficult it still is to be an out, male, and feminine. Even as Christian nationalists and their Republican legislative attack drag performances in states everywhere, none of them even bothers to *mention* male crossdressers, although the total number of drag queens is a small rounding error on this population. At a time of when LGBTQ+ are out and proud, with a few exceptions (I'm looking at *You, Ciara Cremin*) crossdressing remains the trans identity that dares not speak its name.

Second, transsexuals are generally afforded at least some (tenuous) social and political legitimacy. LGBTQ+ groups and even some women's organizations go to bat for us, and the Democratic Party often at least gestures toward doing so as well.

But in spite of their large presence under the trans umbrella, no organization or political group speaks about crossdressers at all. In fact, not even national *transgender* organizations do so. People may say "transgender rights" or "transgender people," but none of them is ever talking about the straight male crossdressers who make up the bulk of our community and were the point of origin for the trans rights movement.

Finally, unlike transsexuals, who might be feared or loathed, crossdressers are almost universally considered simply figures for ridicule. Men in dresses are nearly always a punchline on both sides of the political spectrum.[116] Unlike changing your pronouns or your gender or your genitalia, crossdressing is simply considered unserious just as transitioning for sexual reasons. Thus does academic discomfort with and the intellectual disrepute in which trans sexuality is held limit and deform the study of trans lives.

Early in my transition, when I would go out in full femme, if someone misgendered me as "Sir," I would be totally humiliated, afraid that they thought I was a crossdresser. I would have this irresistible impulse to explain to them that I was not "just a crossdresser," but a *transsexual*, someone legit. And I was all dolled up because it *was my identity*—not because I got off on women's underwear or I enjoyed wearing women's clothing. And all this blatant internalized cross-phobia was from a then-leader (supposedly) in the national trans movement.

But then—along with sexuality—gender expression has always been an unloved stepchild of trans studies in a field relentlessly focused on valorizing gender identity. Although almost every transsexual and many others under the transgender umbrella begin their transition by adopting clothing and body styles (hair, adornment, etc.) generally associated with "the opposite sex," we devote almost no serious attention to gender expression.

Shortly after the end of the Lesbian Sex Wars, proto-TERF anti-sex lesbians, who had recently been denouncing butch-femmes as derivative, artificial, and heterocentric, had already begun pivoting to level similar accusations against trans women. A prominent member of the pro-sex crowd, a renowned high-femme lesbian activist, was a featured presenter at a speak-out for Camp Trans.

Her opening statement silenced the room, unambiguously declaring the importance of gender expression, demanding respect for it, and valorizing its inextricable connection to erotic embodiment, desire, sexuality, and identity:

I'm not a lesbian femme because I look this way naturally. My hair isn't naturally blond, and my lips aren't naturally red. I am a femme because I want to feel a butch's weight on my back and feel a butch moving inside me. And I demand that my erotic desires and choices be recognized and respected as such and as my human right.

Erotic Privilege

Disability scholars have coined the term "lens of desirability" to refer to the politics of a person's sexual desirability to others. In *Trans Sex*, Lucie suggests that to this we add to the portmanteau *desire-ability* to capture the politics of an individual's own capacity to experience sexual desire and pleasure.[117]

Trans studies has devoted a lot of scholarly energy to analyzing *passing privilege*, particularly regarding the politics of visibility in public spaces. Fielding calls those who can access both *desirability* and *desire-ability* as having *erotic privilege*. (This is very close to what gender studies psychologist Deborah Tolman' called *sexual subjectivity*—being able to experience one's self as a sexual being who is entitled to pleasure, who can exercise sexual agency, and who identifies as a sexual being.[118])

When it comes to having erotic privilege, the trans subject may be caught in a lose-lose position: either being hypersexualized or fetishized as a sex object, or else rejected as a *bad object* for erotic engagement. As the writer Brody put it in the *Trans Sex Zine* essay

"Desirability," when contemplating their own impending physical transition, "I felt like I was making a choice between the possibilities of finding comfort and pride in my body, and anyone wanting to fuck me."[119]

Like passing privilege, erotic privilege intersects with factors like race, class, age, and disability. And trans people—pre-op, non-op, post-op, binary and nonbinary—have experiences of arousal, pleasure, and sexual intimacy that are often highly complex. Yet our theory seldom engages with this—a process Fielding terms *flattening out*. Such flattening applies to all three levels of intimate interaction: our response to our sexual embodiment, our partner's response to us, and our bodies' sexual response and function in intimacy.

All of these are to some degree contingent and socially constructed in important ways, and all are affected to a greater or a lesser degree by ciscentrism. We tend to think of sex as a "natural" bodily function. But stripped of its normative boundaries, it is anything but. Fielding draws on a scene from the television series, *Star Trek: The Next Generation*, in which Lt. Cmdr. Data—an android—is asked by a prospective female partner: "You *are* fully functional, aren't you?"[120] The nonplussed Data stammers an awkward response in the affirmative.

This is an excellent metaphor for how many of the trans people feel when confronted with intimacy with prospective cisgender or even transgender erotic partners, and the sometimes complex negotiations that can entail about what equipment is available and how it functions (or doesn't), how we want them named and understood, what we want to do with them, and what we want to have done to them.

Asexual Identity: Just Not a Sexual Identity

What happens to the sex of transsexual when it becomes transgender? Is sex a site of world building for trans politics or thinking now?[121]

—AREN Z. AIZURA ("THINKING WITH TRANS NOW")

Sexual orientation is who you go to bed with, gender identity is who you go to bed as.

—[POPULAR EXPLANATION OF SEXUAL
ORIENTATION VS. GENDER IDENTITY]

While trans studies continues to be written with great insight about gender identity and the many harms of ciscentrism, it has tended to treat the trans person themselves as a neutered subject, stripped of all the erotic and entirely physical desires that motivate some of us (at least in part) to undergo our transitions in the first place. My recent search of Google Scholar on "transgender" and "sexuality" returned just three articles—two of them from Nature and one from Emerald Publishing, and none from the traditional LGBTQ+ or critical studies journals.[122]

One recent meta-analysis found that among 6,000+ peer-reviewed studies that mentioned sexuality in regard to trans subjects, almost all of this was a passing mention in works focused on gay people, and just 2 percent of these studies actually interrogated actual sexual behavior.[123] My guess is that of those that did so, many were probably about HIV, which is where trans sexuality most often surfaces as a topic of scholarly interest.

From this perspective, I've watched with interest the many recent declarations by trans academics in various journals that the field must reengage with our "actual lives." As theorist Paisley Currah has noted, some trans scholars are beginning to "focus not on the open-endedness of trans, or its ability to disassemble [gender], but on the experiences and needs—from abysmal to joyful, from mundane to divine—of actual trans people."[124] But in pieces that do this, I always look to see if the writer has avoided mentioning sex, and I'm almost never disappointed.

For example, Vivian Namaste's entirely admirable call in *Sex Change, Social Change: Reflections on Identity, Institutions, and Imperialism* for a trans studies that addresses the real problems with which many trans people wrestle, such as police violence, accessing to medical care, securing jobs, or finding housing says little about trans people's all-too-common struggles with desire, sex, intimacy, or simply dating.[125] One does not have to become a cheerleader for monogamous marriage and the hetero-nuclear family to acknowledge that many trans people seek for a satisfying sex life with someone they love and the closeness offered by long-term romantic intimacy.

Similarly, in "After Trans Studies," Harsin Drager and Chu provide a moving shopping list of the ordinary and very pedestrian things many transsexual women hope for on the other side of surgery: "cunt, a man, a house, . . . a dishwasher . . . and a normal fucking life." But they never mention that many of us also hope for "a life of normal fucking"—as if sex is an afterthought, not something that trans people do or should desire, and our partners and spouses objects only for our platonic affections.[126]

As Fielding explains, simply enjoying *normal fucking* can be a huge challenge for many, perhaps even *most*, trans people. It is not just that our postsurgical bodies can be quite complex for us and for others to experience and/or operate, but even what might be considered "normal sexuality" is often also deeply influenced by cisgender aesthetic and functional ideals. Complicating matters further, one study of nearly 1,000 cis and LGBTQ+ people found that almost nine-out-of-ten (87.5 percent) would not consider a transgender person as someone to engage with romantically.[127]

Trans sexuality has always been an academically conflicted site of inquiry. As Chu noted in her piece, "Wanting Bad Things," transsexuality was originally considered a sexual category, an erotic project on the part of hyperfeminine homosexuals who wanted feminine lives and socially acceptable (vaginal) sex with males.[128] Then, Harry Benjamin, a leader in founding trans medicine, proposed that transsexual (women) were actually sexually inert with "no over sex life at all."[129] Today's TERFs have weirdly inverted this, proposing that transsexual women are hypermasculine *heterosexual* men seeking sex with cis women.

Such anti-trans discourses around trans feminine sexuality has tended to oscillate between two opposing poles. As Natalie Reed identifies these as "the 'eunuch'/'rapist' dynamic [in which] trans women were either divorced from any sexual agency of their own [and] functioned as a blank slate onto which cis fantasies may be projected—or else shunted into a variation of the 'pathetic transsexual' ... who is mutilated or had their 'dick cut off' or otherwise is now less than what we were, not simply physically, but in terms of sexuality ... " and our erotic potential.[130]

"Wanting Bad Things" was the first trans piece I'd read in years that devoted such attention to desire. But like other trans pieces, it never addressed actually having sex per se, viewing Chu's lusty lesbian desires mainly as an extension of her desires for affirming surgery. So even in the act of desiring sex, we are always producing some kind of narrative about our gender identity. Even her *New York Times* op-ed was really about gender identity, since it is mostly devoted to her surgery and her dysphoria and has nothing to say about the vagina that she is so certain will not make her happy or provide her with pleasure.[131]

As Billy Huff has noted in "Thinking Trans Sex," trans people seeking care have historically had to "articulate their desire to transition in terms purely associated with (white) gender, thus constructing themselves as virtually asexual."[132] This helped clinicians distinguish them from that reliable sexual fetishist, the Transvestite, or from gay men in search of culturally acceptable sex. Even today, "social acceptance dictates that trans people are seen as (white) upstanding citizens . . . not sexual perverts who . . . alter their bodies for sexual pleasure." So it is okay if I want a vagina for reasons of my identity, because *I'm a woman inside*, but it is perverse if I want it for the pleasure of having *a woman inside me*.

Such pressures have undoubtedly had an effect. But given the scores of articles being published by trans academics yearly now, it hardly seems compelling to lay the blame for the field's continued elision of pleasure and desire entirely at their feet.

Whatever the cause(s), it feels like trans scholarship has largely bought into the idea that the transgender subject must forever be divorced from its sexuality, implicitly utilizing the homonormative distinction between sex/gayness and gender/trans. This neutering of the trans subject is especially unfortunate given what a crucial area sex is for understanding and documenting the trans experience, and how many of us struggle with sex, with romance, and with arousal both before and after whatever bodily changes we might undergo.

I wonder—can trans theorists ever speak publicly about our bodies or desires in any register that is not connected to explicating our dysphoria or validating our gendered identities? Surely gendered dysphoria and the desire for affirmative embodiment are key reasons many of us seek out our various body modifications and affirming care.

But bodies *do* things. And different kinds of bodies do *different* kinds of things. They create the possibility of experiencing different kinds of erotic embodiment as well different kinds of arousal, pleasure, and fulfillment.[133] Biology may not be destiny, but it often *is* function.

Do *all* of us get genital surgery strictly for reasons of identity or dysphoric and discursive relief, and *none* for the more brute and mechanical things we hope our new genitalia can *do* during intimacy? Do none of us go through surgery simply because we want, not just our bodies, but for sex itself to finally *feel right*, for our bodies to finally be able to perform the acts and intimacies that we find arousing, even fulfilling?

The academic silence surrounding this topic also contributes to deforming the discourse around genital surgery. Much of our future sex lives lie in the hands (and prejudices) of our surgeons, and the technical decisions they make, especially when (a) their post-op priorities might be wildly out of line with ours, and (b) we're never been encouraged to talk about our hopes and goals about postoperative sex.[134]

Surgeons often don't devote nearly as much attention to our post-op sexual possibilities and sensations (among trans women anyway) as they do to the cosmetic appearance and the ability to accommodate intromission by a penis—a factor certainly not high on my own personal hit parade. As I wrote in Read My Lips, I was almost denied surgery by my team at the Cleveland Clinic because I insisted on functional clitoris, rather than the purely cosmetic extrusion they had planned, which they misinterpreted as ambivalence about losing my penis.[135]

When I tried to point out to them that, as a lesbian, a clitoris seemed like it might be a handy thing to have postoperatively, they canceled my impeding surgery and told me to take another year (!). Then my op-ed about this was rejected by the New York Times: "My New Clitoris Won't Make Me Happy (But It Would Still Be Nice to Have One)." As Sandra Mesics wrote about her own impending surgery with admirable understatement in "Building a Better Vulva": "I really would have liked to have an orgasm now and then."[136]

I suspect my surgical team would have entirely different reactions, had I told them that I was worried that the many hot men I hoped to have post-op sex with might be put off by a strictly cosmetic clitoris. Or if I demanded more vaginal depth to ensure I could accommodate them fully. Because these would have been "acceptable" heterocentric qualms. But a trans woman focused on her clitoris rather than her vagina must have something wrong.[137]

As Eric Plemons has noted, "cishetero penetrative intercourse structures surgeons' conception of, techniques for, and desired outcomes of surgical procedures; they are evaluated for their social, not their sensation-producing, features."[138] In similar vein, surgeons will often still reject trans men who elect to retain their clitoris and vagina because of their valorizing of the cis-normative body.[139] Today, the more sophisticated surgeons are slowly changing this, but as Plemons notes, surgeons work from understandings of postoperative transgender body that are guided by and prioritize the cisgender imaginary.

This focus away from pleasure and gratification as a site of surgical interest and as a site of academic investment reflect a common underlying problem: all transsexual desires and passions must be banished except for the passionate desire for personal and social alignment with one's gender identity.

Certainly, it is the only reputable and respectable desire cissociety allows us. We don't talk about other desires, and for all the sexualized objectification of transsexuals, cisgender people don't talk about them either. Only gendered identities—asexual and antiseptic—will do.

In this regard, it is encouraging to see some trans scholars attempting to refocus trans studies away from traditional tropes of dysphoric pain, to counternarratives of "gender joy" and "gender euphoria." Yet although this sounds promising at first, its confined to the "satisfaction and joy [of] numerous gender affirming experiences."[140,141] So even "gender joy" and "gender euphoria" must be left at the door to the bedroom, the products of psychological, rather than physical or erotic, pleasures.

I can't be the only trans person who has sometimes welcomed the relief of orgasm in which, for at least a moment, all the complexities of my body and the myriad meanings with which it has been freighted, and their associated pains and confusion, all dissolve into brief moment of trans ecstasy—a very different and fleshy "gender euphoria" than the thrill of gender identity affirming experiences. But then, arousal and orgasm still remain too conflicted, too contested, and too personally problematic for trans scholarship to interrogate— even as they remain very real sites for gender joy, resistance, and empowerment in everyday transgender lives.

The Promise of Ecstasy?

We are a horny bunch. . . . Yet I cannot deny that de-sexualized undercurrents have risen to the surface of trans advocacy. . . . My essays attempt to put the sex back in transsexual.[142]

—FLORENCE ASHLEY (

*Gender/Fucking: The Pleasures and Politics of Living in a Gendered Body)*The time has come to talk about sex.[143]

—GAYLE RUBIN (THINKING SEX: NOTE FOR A RADICAL
THEORY OF SEXUAL POLITICS)

Yet I still harbor hopes that, as the irreplaceable Gayle Rubin once declared, it *is* time for us to at last talk about sex.

I want to return to Hollibaugh and Moraga's question of *who we're rolling around in bed with,* what we want to do with them, and what we want them to do to us. Since "[t]his most privatized aspect of ourselves, our sex lives, has dead-ended into silence," what might catalyze the emergence of more robust academic attention not trans sexuality?

The critical reckoning among lesbian feminist academic provoked by the Sex Wars—of which Hollibaugh and Moraga's piece was emblematic—resulted from the kind of vigorous public conflict over *politically incorrect sex* that the trans community has so far been spared. We've never had to wrestle with the public condemnations of an explicitly anti-sex/anti-porn/anti-prostitution wing, and, in retrospect, perhaps not having to defend or interrogate our sexuality has not been an unalloyed good.

The Sex Wars produced foundational, even astonishing thinking about the politics of women's sexuality and desire. Eventually this opened up profound new areas of critical thought about sexual agency as a site not only of feminine pleasure, danger, and resistance.

On the other side, a vociferous anti-sex coalition rolled BD/SM, butch/fem roles, rape, porn, commercial sex work, sexual harassment, date rape, and any sex that eroticized power into what Butler has called a *copula*, in which all were considered equal and equally oppressive.[144]

Janet Halley, in her book, *Split Decisions: How and Why to Take a Break from Feminism*, offers a perfect example of this rhetorical trick, quoting noted anti-sex warrior Katherine MacKinnon declaring:[145]

[T]he way subordination is done in pornography is the way it is done in prostitution is the way it is done in the rest of the world: rape, battering, sexual abuse of children, sexual harassment, and murder are sold in prostitution and are the acts out of which pornography is made. To make distinctions is to be fooled by male domination.

In this vein, anti-sex feminists would assert that butch-femme couples were merely imitating the oppressive power dynamics of heterosexuality in which men dominated women in a kind of symbolic rape which was the basis of actual rape and thus not very different from consensual lesbian BD/SM, and so on.

Many of the same anti-sex feminists are now anti-trans TERFs, and once again make a *copula* of transsexuality in which transsexual women are aping "real women" by appropriating their body parts so they can invade women's spaces, which is a kind of symbolic rape similar to actual rape that natal male predators seek to inflict on natal women, and on and on. It is a kind of linguistic terrorism that chains a "parade of horribles" to whatever group or minority they seek to villainize.

As a baby *tranny* lesbian still getting kicked out of NYC women's groups, I was privileged to attend the East Village speak-out by many of the pro-sex lesbians who had been silenced at Barnard that was organized by the Lesbian Sex Mafia. (Ironically, just a decade later, the Transexual Menace would picket LSM for its trans-exclusionary policies. LSM kindly offered to amend their policy to "post-ops only," but the Menace was having none of that dish, either.)

It would turn out to be a veritable *Who's Who* of pro-sex lesbian/feminist theorists who would transform their field over the coming three decades. Along with Moraga and Hollibaugh, this included Dorothy Allison (*Bastard Out of Carolina*, etc.), Joan Nestle (*Persistent Desire*, etc.), Patrick Califia (*Coming to Power*, etc.), Ester Newton (*Mother Camp*, etc.), Gayle Rubin (*The Traffic in Women*, etc.), Sarah Shulman (*Rat Bohemia*, etc.), Carole Vance (*Pleasure and Danger*, etc.), bell hooks (*Ain't I a Woman?*, etc.), and a young Judith Butler (no books that I could find, but I hear they're big overseas).[146,147]

For these women and others like Jewell Gomez, Audre Lorde, Minnie Bruce Pratt, a young and then-obscure trans masc individual named Leslie Fienberg (*Stone Butch Blues*), theorizing "sexual fulfillment was a means of learning about oneself, a way to deepen intimate relationships, and as a technique of resistance and survival."[148] Declared one theorist with characteristic blunt defiance, "We are the women who like to come and come hard."

This was a new voice demanding that women's sexual agency be taken seriously without the artificial limits imposed by the necessity of being *politically correct*, including butch-femme roles, BD/SM, strap-ons, anonymous encounters, and all the rest. It was, as theorist Jack Halberstam has put it, "a discourse of acts rather than identities," addressing the kinds of sexual narratives that those of us who must fight for erotic purchase in an often-unfriendly and uncomprehending world must invent, improvise, and even force into existence.[149]

In other words, it was a discourse that refused to see lesbian sexes and genders as merely the play of meaning upon the body's surface but as something much deeper and more urgent, and as exceeding the bounds of philosophic abstraction to reek of the sweat of lesbian desire and arousal.

But trans people have been part of the BD/SM scene for too long for that kink to produce any kind of productive intellectual conflict. And too many of us have had to turn to commercial sex as our main income for a serious anti-prostitution/anti-porn movement to emerge. And of course gender role-play is practically definitional for being trans-identified.

So trans academia has avoided the sort of communal conflict over sexuality that might have fed a Trans Sex War and forced it to address issues of sexuality more directly. It appears there is nothing on the horizon that might finally move trans academics into a more direct engagement with sexuality and erotic embodiment as a privileged site of interest.

So the question is perhaps not will trans theory, like lesbian/ feminist theory, ever develop a "pro-sex wing," but rather will trans theory ever develop a "sex wing" at all? This is not an unimportant question. As Cherrie Moraga wrote: "Most of us harbor demons and old hurts inside ourselves around sexuality . . . [and] what we keep private and hidden often becomes painful and deformed." This is also true in spades for many transgender people. We who still know in our bones the secret we no longer speak aloud but can only whisper alone in the dark—*there is no point in transition without the promise of ecstasy—because we are the women who like to come, and come hard.*

2

Bodies Do Things/ Things Done to Bodies

Welcome to "Caveat Hell"

I stated at the beginning of this book that I didn't think I'd ever read a transgender academic study that dealt directly and frankly with the experience of postsurgical sex, on crucial topics like the quality of postoperative arousal and orgasm, on the challenges of reconnecting one's sexuality, sexual practice, and sense of erotic embodiment with all the complexities inherent in suddenly having a new postoperative genitalia.

Other than an abortive attempt some decades ago in a regrettably named chapter titled, "Our Cunts Are NOT the Same," I haven't done so either.[1] So I would like to make that long overdue attempt here.

Engaging in Jamesian introspection of one's body, emotions, or intimate acts is never going to offer anything like the clean intellectual bite of deconstructing a text or critiquing a theory. Writing about internal states is extremely "mushy" intellectually and can end up wandering around their subject while also proving pretty embarrassing for its author.

Unfortunately, nothing that follows will be any exception. However, I have tried wherever possible to connect personal and phenomenological observation with theory—perhaps closer to what communications theorists Boylorn and Orbe call "critical autoethnography," which "moves beyond simply documenting an experience to deconstructing it through theorization and critical analysis."[2]

While I am not interested in producing another story of origins beginning with that deathless line of transgender prose—"Ever since I was a fully fertilized embryo, I always . . . "—I have utilized something like this narrative structure in a few places where I have experiences that originated so early as to complicate, if not confound, claims of being discursively constructed. I do this because I think this feels like an important ontological point—not to validate any gender claims (which I don't make anyway).

Language about bodies is always tricky, and gendered or sexual language doubly so since so many words are overloaded with meaning, highly politicized, and open to multiple and even adverse interpretation. So a long list of caveats follows.

I'm aware that "vagina" only refers the genital canal, and not the entirety of the feminine genitals. With that said, I will use the two largely interchangeably in order to avoid "cunt," "pussy," or the archaic and laboratory-inflected "pudenda."

Nothing here should be read as equating *womanhood* with *vagina* or *penetration*. If one were to construct a logical syllogism around this, it might read as follows: not all women have vaginas; not all who have vaginas (or *front holes*) are women; not all who are women or who have vaginas desire penetration; and not all those who desire penetration are women or have vaginas.

Penetration is not a necessary part of sex and when it is— regardless of the orifice involved—it need not be an act of submission, vulnerability, or femininely gendered. Bodily orifices and their penetration can be understood as active, masculine, a means of surrounding and actively engulfing or of controlling or dominating an intimate encounter. Even submissiveness itself can paradoxically also be part of dominating or controlling an erotic encounter. Or as a tee-shirt I once saw in a Greenwich Village window read, "Rule from the bottom—or not at all!"

Nothing about bodies, orifices, or intimate acts need necessarily be gendered at all, much less the way I will here—although, for some of us, therein lies much of the pleasure. For example, as author/ publisher Trystan Cotten notes, many trans men are happy and satisfied with their *manhole, manvagina, bonus holes, frontholes, or boycunts.*[3] Presumably, they instantiate their orifices and any intimate acts in which they engage differently than I do, or are aroused by different erotic narratives of them. Morphology, too, is not always destiny.

I'm also clear that many of my own experiences and attendant judgments are overly dark. I often read and see online (I'm looking at *you*, WeHappyTrans.com) about trans people who find the experience of being trans pleasing, or are happy with being trans and exactly the state in which their bodies arrived. While I admire such views and am deeply envious of them, unfortunately I can muster absolutely nothing in my own experience that even remotely resonates with this.

For me, it was not just a matter of the *mindfuck shitshow of transition* but also those two *other* mindfuck shitshows: a nightmarish pre-transition childhood and a long and difficult post-transition adaptation to a changed body.

I use the word "woman" or "trans woman" for descriptive shorthand in a world in which I recognize my own sense of gendered embodiment, and many of my body parts and some small portion of my personal characteristics have been considered traditionally feminine and/or associated with females. Forced to make a choice in the binary world in which I'm apparently going to live out my days, I still use the Women's Room and tend to prefer being called she/her—but neither of these are necessarily deal-breakers. I would very much prefer not to have to make any choice at all—about the genders of my bathrooms or my body—and in the genderqueer world to come I would happily relinquish both.

Finally, I don't believe whatever form of embodiment I have or have acquired *makes me a woman*—whether in my own mind or the minds of others, before or after whatever medical procedures I may have undergone. I am also not particularly invested in the term "woman," and certainly not in "transsexual" or "transgender."

Sex and the Transsexed Body

Sex and its physical embodiment were once the sine qua non of what was called "transsexuality"—before the term became politically injudicious in some quarters because, as an irritated nonbinary youth explained to me with pained patience, "It genitalizes gender."

But *genitalizing gender* was precisely the point of my own transition, and I devoted tens of thousands of dollars and about a decade of my life in pursuit of it. I not only had surgery on my genital area because I wanted to bring it "into alignment with my gender identity," but also for the more messy and urgent reason of wanting to have vaginal sex—specifically to be penetrated by women, rather than the other way around.

Somehow, before I even knew there *was* such a thing, I wanted a vagina—or at least a vagina-like organ. I would stand naked before my parents' full-length bedroom mirror, transfixed by idea of penetration, even as I was dimly aware that the only kind I was able to do with my finger was vaguely uncomfortable and not at all satisfying. I'm sure I didn't know *what* I wanted, so I played with my butt a lot while feeling frustrated by the result. Not that it didn't have its pleasant aspects, but it just wasn't what I had in mind, whatever that might be.

Interestingly, for any Freudians among us, none of this was directly connected with sex: I didn't know that sex existed, and certainly had never had an erotic impulse or sexual interaction with anyone or anything (including my front organ). So I connect my fascination with the idea of penetration with the idea that I might be an act *between people* or something that someone might do *to me* or that I might to do to others. And given the poverty of my physical and sexual knowledge, I certainly didn't connect it to "girl" or to the classic *wrong body* sense of dysphoria (yet).[4]

In other words, nothing in it was related so-called *object relations*, or, as Bettcher puts it, "awareness of oneself as an object for others" as a means of romantic intimacy.[5]

But I knew something was very wrong. As Bettcher puts it (in a different context), "The question isn't 'What's wrong with me?' The question, rather, is part of a more general 'What the hell is going on here?'"[6]

When I finally discovered my penis as something other than a urinary organ, my earliest fumbling encounters with self-pleasure all treated it as something more like a large clitoris-type organ. I was still ignorant of female anatomy, and so the connection wouldn't have occurred to me. But I did everything with it *but* the common, masculine jacking-off motion in which I had no interest. In fact, I tended to ignore the shaft and focused instead on developing several very inventive if somewhat unsatisfying ways of playing with the sensitive tip.

A decade later, when I finally had my first real girlfriend, I taught her to do these things, too. I also taught her to push my legs apart while doing it, which was very erotic to me for reasons I couldn't fathom. I was still hiding from the idea that I was trans, so while I didn't identify this as dysphoria per se, I was aware of being immensely frustrated with the things my body couldn't do and very unsatisfied with the things that it could.

Everything I wanted to do or that seemed erotic to me kept happening on other people's (women's) bodies. Which brings me back to the argument about functionality and eroticism being an important, if usually unmentioned, part of the desire to transition, and assertion that not all of us pursue transition solely to relieve dysphoria or realize gender alignment.

My unusual sexual behaviors persisted through my adult years of preoperative sex with (cisgender) women. Without realizing it, I focused my erotic attention on pretty much everything one could do with a *girldick* except the kinds of things most other penis-bearing individuals seemed to be doing with theirs. As Lucie Fielding would write in *Trans Sex*, "When a partner plays with my clit (the term I use for my genitalia), pumping or jerking motions tend to be intensely distressing, whereas flicking or swirling motions feel yummy and allow me to drop back into my body and be present."

My own experiences were not the same, but they were similar, and if all this was not fulfilling, at least it was physically pleasurable. This provided an answer to the age-old TERF taunt: *Why do trans women need surgery—can't they just treat their penises like big clitorises?*

It turns out I *could*, after a fashion, and I *did*—and I'm sure many pre-op and non-op trans women do so much more satisfactorily than I. As Hale and Bettcher have pointed out, trans people can and often do engage in complex activities and fantasies to lessen their dysphoria and facilitate being intimate with body parts by mentally retooling and recoding them. [7,8] But as Hale notes, there can be limits to this "reconstituting the sexualized social spaces of our bodies . . . [and] we cannot ourselves reconfigure the social meanings of certain bodily zones."

While he is certainly right that there are limits to how much we can reconfigure the external social meanings of our body parts, I don't think there's theoretically any limit to doing so privately. While I certainly reached the limits of my own reconfiguration abilities— or desire to—it seems to me that Fielding does a pretty good job in this regard. There is likely wide variation among trans people in this regard that we have yet to explore.

While I don't think there's any ontological reason that, say, penises must feel or signify masculinity and vaginas must feel and signify femininity, there are probably some biological anchors for this somewhere, and probably any number of discursively mandated reasons for our experiencing them this way. But that doesn't necessarily mean there's anything inherently gendered in these or other bodily features (more on this later in the section on aesthetics).

On the other hand, if there aren't many hardwired semiotic limits to this retooling, there certainly are personal ones, and I had run up against my own.

And also functional ones: while my girldick might have been a kind of clitoris for me, that didn't mean it functioned the same way as that *other* clitoris. The physical mechanics and the sensations were clearly in a different register, and I found myself constantly eroticizing things it couldn't do and confused and unsatisfied by the things it could. I had no interest in using my own girldick for penetration, and—with all due respect to those who "pack" or get phalloplasties—it always felt *in my way* during sex, an obstructive between myself and my partner that perversely became more so the more I got aroused.

In addition, there was nothing my girldick could do that would substitute for the functional possibilities created by having a vagina. While pleasuring the outside of a girldick and the inside of a vagina might be somewhat similar, they are structurally and erotically very, very different experiences for me. And I couldn't escape the sense of being a kind of morphological failure during sex, especially when compared to the women I was with.

This puts to bed another TERF-y question: "*If bodies are socially constructed, then instead of surgery, you should just change the discourse.*"

Of course, no one can change a discourse, particularly one in which one is embedded. But even if the body is largely constructed, as

Butler has explained, this doesn't mean we can all pick up whichever gendered body we want off the rack every morning and wear a different one each day.

The fact that something is socially constructed does not necessarily imply that individuals are empowered to change it to suit themselves. Money is entirely a social construction but no individual can change that either.

Certainly, allowing more ways to *think the body* would be welcome to those of us who are dysphoric. Preoperatively, I can't tell you how many of these same TERFs would point to the presence of my penis as a means to humiliate and stigmatize me. Certainly, TERFs changing *their own* discourse would be immensely helpful to trans people's dysphoria.

But even if we could change the discourse at will, social construction and personal retooling only get you so far. As was said earlier, different kinds of bodies *do* different kinds of things. We give them different meanings; we eroticize them differently, and they provide the possibility for desiring different kinds of acts and experiencing different kinds of pleasure.

With all that said, I am certain that there are many trans women for whom the physical pleasures available from having an *outie* are neither more nor less available to them phenomenologically than those of having an *innie*. I do wonder if they aren't at least different.

I'm also sure that many trans women and crossdressers find their own girldicks entirely fulfilling and fine as they are. Fielding and Cremin, respectively, seem to be examples of these.

Finally, I am also confident that for many trans women the fleshy materiality of vaginas and breasts are not necessary for feeling a proper sense of gendered embodiment.

It just happens that, unfortunately, none of these include me.

Weighing Anchors

While I largely agree with Butlerian propositions about gender—such as that the binary-ness of both sex and gender as constructed, that sex is already gendered way of looking at bodies, that we become coherent social beings through understanding ourselves as gendered and sexed subjects, and there is no *body* prior to its signification—I also recognize that it is impossible to situate the entirety my own experience of sexed embodiment within the theoretical space they provide.

Paraphrasing Gayle Rubin's observation in *Thinking Sex*, perhaps no single theory can or should be expected to provide *the ultimate and complete account* of gender.[9]

Although undoubtedly constructed, gender is a complex system whose many intricacies are unlikely to be fully exhausted by any one theoretical approach—even one as powerful as Butler's.

The transsexed subject can be both discursively formed through performative gendered acts constrained by some prior gendered interiority. There is a middle ground somewhere between trans studies valorizing the interiority and essential nature of gendered identities, and queer theory's refusal to acknowledge anything as being outside of or prior to discourse.

I'm not sure these two projects are as mutually exclusive as theorists often seem to want them to be, any more than our interminable arguments over nature versus nurture. Or as Henry Rubin declares,

"[I]n the study of bodies and subjectivity . . . Foucauldian discourse analysis is not incompatible with phenomenology . . . phenomenology and genealogy are complementary methods that augment one another's strengths."[10,11]

Yet Rubin also pinpoints the distinct tension between the two, one that has continued to bedevil trans studies as both are positioned within and positioned in opposition to queer theory:

> Foucault's discursive method tends to undermine the authority of the individual speaking subjects and thereby plays into patterns of domination that work against the possibility of marginalized subjects using their knowledge of their own subject positions to speak counter-discursively. . . . [P]henomenology legitimates the knowledge of the subject, while pointing out the critical possibilities that result from the subject's negotiation with the world.[12]

And it is precisely through this phenomenonologic sense of self that the trangender self emerges, which grounds the entire trangender project. Thus, as Keagan notes, "trans studies has long been concerned with narratology—with the project of locating narrative structures that will adequately allow for the existence of trans bodies and becomings."[13] (I would only add that cis people often create similar body narratives.)

So while the phenomenologic sense of our bodies is critical to the trans self, queer theory demands of us a certain skepticism toward it, and toward essentializing either that sense or the narratives woven from it. It is a difficult balancing act.

(And of course, it often means eroticism is pushed aside, or, as Bettcher poignantly puts it, "[O]ne is so busy looking to provide a theoretical frame of reference that will render trans people intelligible [that] the question about trans sexuality . . . disappears."[14])

I'm reminded of the opposition between classical Newtonian physics and quantum physics, where the former perfectly describes the behavior of large object, while the latter perfectly describes the behavior of subatomic ones. Even though mathematically incompatible, physics needs and uses both to describe material reality. Even that smartphone in your pocket needs and uses both every time you turn it on.

Similarly, it's not so much that phenomenological perception of the trans self and social construction theory are in conflict, but are necessary parts of a whole. Transsexual and Transgender are undoubtedly constructed categories of identity, but they rest on at least some nonzero amount of raw phenomenological and/or biological ingredients on which social construction has acted.[15]

Thus, my own phenomenological experiences keep leading me back to at least some of what Riki Lane called a "clear neurological correlate"—one that is something less than 100 percent reduceable to discourse.[16]

How else do I explain a desire for a vagina-type opening in my genital area which was clearly *not* my anus to my eight-or-nine-year-old self? And my seemingly instinctive desire to play with my girldick as a clitoris, when I didn't know such an organ existed? And my corresponding disinterest in "jacking-off" with it and the idea of penetration?

Moreover, I'm at a loss to think of any external organ on my body that I could have had to thoroughly reconfigure surgically with such resulting phenomenological satisfaction—let alone something as central to my body, identity, and sexual functioning as my genitals.

I am also unable to think of any other significant body part which could be so drastically reconfigured and still add, rather than subtract, from my sense of self and comfort in my body—not to mention my enjoyment of sex.

What else but some sort of biological anchor could explain the seven-year-old me—who didn't know the word "vagina" or that such an organ existed, and who was still unaware of intercourse, much less that vaginal penetration could be a part of it, and who was nonetheless intensely interested in an act she had not heard of performed with an organ she neither possessed nor knew existed? And that somehow all of *this* was "socially constructed" through discursive practices to which she had not yet been exposed?

In a similar vein, post-transition I was once asked by a trans male friend if I didn't "miss that weight up front." I know this is a sentence in English, but I have no referent for its meaning. He might as well have asked me if I missed levitating or turning invisible. This had always been true: something in me failed to identify with this most intimate of identificatory organs from a very early age.

I also don't see any way to argue that such interiority is *both* discursively formed and yet also—in the case of transsexed children— contravenes and refutes the very discourses that are alleged to have constituted it, discourses which are also among our culture's most pervasive, intrusive, and implacable.

Otherwise we end up in one of the those *Heads-I-win/Tails-you-lose* double-binds common in postmodernism's *paranoid style*, in which if one accepts their subject position, it shows the power of discourse, but on other hand if one rejects their subject position, that *really* proves the power of discourse, if only by opposition, since *any* subjectivity is de facto a product of discourse.

Such a position leaves us with the Butler's "Undoing Gender" in which subjects are resigned to their own discursive construction, reduced to brief moments of individual parodic and ironic repetition as their sole means of resistance. This may make for good philosophy, but it sounds an awful lot like a prescription for isolation and powerlessness.

Another argument for some kind of biological correlate comes from the fact that those of us who pursue gender-affirming surgeries tend to pursue very narrow range of outcomes. I'm not aware of anyone who, by requesting bottom surgery, has done so in pursuit of any genital organ than what would not be usually understood in terms of a penis or a vagina. Nor for organs in places other than their genital area—even though there are presumably many places where one could be constructed. (It is an interesting ontological question whether genital organs in other places would still *be* genital organs, since the location is intrinsic to the identification.)

Many non-op or pre-op trans women and men also still talk about their *pussies* and *dicks/penises*, respectively. For instance, consider these two remarkable passages from subjects in Howitt's "How We Fuck":[17]

My energy-vagina, it's important for me to feel it. When I get fucked by a transguy, transboy or a transgenderbutch, when I get fucked by a person with an energy-dick, I feel and realize the beauty of his/their clitdic/dick. We fuck and it's 100% real. The dick went into my vagina.

I can fuck with a strap on and dildo. In the beginning it's a piece of silicone which gets connected to my vagina with the belts out of leather around my body. If I feel like getting sexual, if the connection is hot enough, the belts of the strap-on are roots which grow in my body which drink from my sexual energy and feed the dildo to grow in to a dick.

Even those of us getting nonbinary surgeries who often refer to themselves as "Salmacians" tend to want a phallus added to an existing vagina or vice versa. They do not request entirely new kinds of genitals or genitals in other areas.[18,19]

I supposed one could still argue that all of these are effects of discourse, but it doesn't feel to me like a compelling or satisfying argument.

Butler themselves seems to acknowledge something along these lines in an interview with Cristan Williams in "TransAdvocate," in which they stumble all over trying not to name the biological anchor, which is clearly being referred to:[20]

We form ourselves within the vocabularies that we did not choose, and sometimes we have to reject those vocabularies, or actively develop new ones. For instance, gender assignment is a "construction" and yet many genderqueer and trans people refuse those assignments in part or in full. That refusal opens the way for a more radical form of self-determination.

The problem with that view of social construction is that it suggests that what trans people feel about what their gender is, and should be, is itself "constructed" and, therefore, not real. And then the feminist police comes along to expose the construction and dispute a trans person's sense of their lived reality. I oppose this use of social construction absolutely, and consider it to be a false, misleading, and oppressive use of the theory.

I know that some subjective experiences of sex are very firm and fundamental, even unchangeable. They can be so firm and unchanging that we call them "innate."

But given that we report on such a sense of self within a social world, a world in which we are trying to use language to express what we feel, it is unclear what language does that most effective. I understand that "innate" is a word that conveys the sense of something hired-wired and constitutive . . . that when people tried to talk that way, they were trying to "fix" a social reality into a natural necessity.

And yet, sometimes we do need a language that refers to a basic, fundamental, enduring, and necessary dimension of who we are, and the sense of sexed embodiment can be precisely that.

As philosophy, this comes perilously close to the word "salad," encapsulating as it does the limitations of postmodernism's suspicion of identificatory practices claimed by abjected minorities whose experiences clearly seem to indicate some sort of prior neurological correlate.

This leaves Butler straddling her own argument: yes, subjectivity is constructed; but no, it also an enduring and unchanging sense of one's gendered embodiment that can be thought of as "innate"—but which is really not. We need language that refers to this, but it certainly can't be "innate." We can call these gendered subjectivities "firm," "basic," "unchanging," "enduring," or "fundamental"—so long as we call them anything *except* "innate."

Butler is trying valiantly here to avoid acknowledging that anything about gendered subjectivity might be pre-discursive.[21] But one does not have to be a fan of biological determinism to agree that we come into the world with at least some nonzero part of us that is inborn or genetic, if only as predispositions or propensities that are then acted upon by discourse and culture.

I suppose I'm holding out here for some limited form of *epistemological individualism* and the proposition that some nonzero fraction of bodily knowledge may not be entirely social but originates with and/or in the individual.

So, we are left where we always are left with sexual minorities: between nature and nature, mining the intersection between individual and discourse. And for those of us who are transsexed, our gendered and sexual embodiment appear to be one of those forms of knowing for which social knowledge is necessary but will never be entirely sufficient.

What Are Emergent Identities Citing?

When Butler characterizes gender as not "a stable identity [but] a stylized repetition of acts," I understand her as referring mostly to "gestures, movements, and enactments of various kinds which constitute the illusion of an abiding gendered self." She does not mean the phenomenological experience of one's body, organs, and sexual desires.

Because postmodernism remains deeply skeptical of the idea of the Self, Butler famously tried to deal with the problem presented by gendered Selves by *embracing the contradiction* and arguing that—yes, there are gendered selves, but one only becomes such a subject by being discursively marked by and recognizing one's self within the gender system.

Put another way, one is not a gendered Self prior to performing the gendered acts that are taken as constituting it.

This is clever, but, like others, I wonder if it's right.

I assume that when Butler wakes up every morning, they know who they are and never mistake themselves for, say, Michel Foucault (although some scholarship asserts otherwise). Doubtless Butler would find it disturbing to learn that someone else was them, or that they were not themselves. ("Butler is a copy for which there is no original"??) I doubt that Butler thinks of themselves as do-ing Judith Butler—what speech-act theory would call a "happy performative." And were I to announce that *I* was Judith Butler, and try to speak as them, that would be an "unhappy performative." (I've actually tried this several times: it never works and *always* leaves me unhappy.)

I don't think epistemically it would make much sense to assert that there is no Judith Butler prior to their emergence as Judith Butler through the repetition of performative acts that cite other Judith Butlers. I think many readers might agree with me if I were to argue that there is really only one Judith Butler, and all others are just pale imitations of the Real.[22]

That is, there *is* a doer behind the deed.

Butler clearly has a deep and long-standing commitment to destabilizing and contesting heterosexual norms through critical theorizing. But without a doer behind the deed, who or what is the site and primary mover of this commitment? Are we to argue that *there is no doer behind this deed, that the Butlerian commitment to liberatory critical theory is performatively constituted by the very academic acts that are said to be its result?*

Similarly, I suspect that Butler, like the Riki I'm performing, finds a certain pleasure in some bodily parts and erotic acts, and others unappealing or even unpleasant. That is, they might find that if they were to be compelled to wear dresses and high heels (something that I've never seen or heard of them doing) or if their body suddenly sprouted lots of chest hair, a beard, and a large phallus, then that would most likely feel strange, uncomfortable, or awkward.

More specifically for the case of postmodernism and queer theory, since Butler now identifies as nonbinary and uses "they/them" drawing on *Gender Trouble*, would we now argue that there is no nonbinary Self prior to performing the nonbinary acts that are taken as constituting it? Or that nonbinary, genderqueer, genderfluid is a performative, a repeated set of acts of within a regulatory frame that produce the appearance of a nonbinary, genderqueer, or genderfluid person?

Does the entire paradigm of social constructionism and Butlerian performativity to which queer theory and much of trans studies are committed really work for sexuality or for emergent nonbinary genders?

For instance, it is unclear to me what prior "copy" Maria Munir was citing and within what regulatory frame when, in 2016, they announced to a perplexed Obama that they were nonbinary—thus becoming the first person most of the world knew as NB. The identity was so new that even Obama, surely one of the best-briefed presidents of my lifetime, had no idea what to make of this information and instead fell back on his gay and transgender talking points. Which was very inclusive of him, but not really relevant to Munir's announcement.

At that time, there was no apparent regulatory "frame" within which to situate Munir's identity, nor were there other apparent performances of it that they appeared to be citing.[23]

One could certainly argue that Munir was making a negative citation *against* the regulatory frame of binary genders, but it's not a particularly satisfying argument to make, especially because (a) it kind of diminishes their identification as merely being reactionary, (b) it does not explain why *this* negative citation when there are nearly many others available (agender, graygender, genderqueer, etc.), and (c) it simply restates the terms of the argument without offering any new information.

My question here is, how does performativity apply to emergent identities? And so far I don't think that Butlerian queer theory has provided any answer.

Disembodied Pleasures

All this returns me to the questions of sexuality and pleasure. As Howitts askes in "How We Fuck," "Why do some sex events trigger catastrophic dysphoria whilst others produce ecstatic pleasure? How does a shift in discourse materially affect, say, orgasm? What makes a set of fleshy topographies stabilise as a clitoris, or a dick, or a manhole?"[24] The question cuts right to my observation about trans body narratives as being stories that also enable us to "read" our own bodies for ourselves. And this becomes the point of reference from which all things trans about us unfold. Or, as Rubin puts it, "Bodies are the ultimate point of view. The body as it exists for oneself is the point of reference by which the whole world unfolds."[25] Adding elsewhere, "We have to perform an immense amount of 'head work' to transport our bodies from the imaginary to the real."[26]

In an early piece addressing their own then-lesbianism, Butler's *Imitation and Gender Subordination* famously observed that "it is precisely the pleasure produced by the instability of these categories which sustains the various erotic practices that make me a candidate for the category to begin with."[27,28]

While sexuality is almost always mediated to some degree through the mind, this is also entirely typical of queer theory: locating erotic pleasure entirely in the intellectual *frisson* of discursive categories, rather than the physical friction of skin against skin and organ on organ. Pleasure here is reduced to a disembodied intellectual exercise.[29,30] And what might these unnamed "erotic practices" be. Butler, like queer theory itself, never specifies any actual physical practices—pleasurable, insubordinate, or otherwise.

The phrase "the pleasure produced" and "sustains practices" are particularly instructive here, since they're in the passive voice, as if the pleasures and practices are disembodied and detached from Butler-as-person. Nowhere in such a sentence is there any indication of a Self who is available to do this desiring or to experience these pleasures.

I confess I am at a loss for how to conceptualize pleasure in this way, without a *do-er behind the deed* that pursues, initiates, and experiences it. One can certainly argue that subject positions like Lesbian and Woman do not exist prior to discourse, and that the experience of desire and pleasure are also constructed in important ways. But it is hard to think of a sexuality or a feeling of erotic desire, absent a experiencing Self in which they originate. Which may be yet another reason why queer theory has tended to avoid engagement with having sex.

Born This Way?

Even if there is an experiencing Self that is entirely discursively constructed, as others have noted, transsexuals are surely among the worst examples of this phenomenon.

Some, perhaps even most, people are not born gendered in any particular way, but come to recognize themselves and their bodies through the gendered discourses to which they are exposed and in which they are situated.

But among these are surely *not* transsexed children, who not only appear to have a fixed sense from age three or four of their genders and bodies but also one that completely *contradicts* the full weight of the powerful discursive forces arrayed against them—including their own family, their school, their religious institution, and the visual evidence of their own flesh.

Serano and Prosser have made similar points in this regard. In her book *Whipping Girl*, Serano declares that "my female subconscious sex was most certainly not the result of socialization or social gender constructs, as it defied everything I had been taught was true about gender, as well as the constant encouragement I received to think of myself as a boy."[31] As Bettcher summarizes: "Given that we move against everything culture has tried to impose on us, how on earth could the basis for our gender unhappiness also be cultural? How could it not be innate?"[32]

One could make similar points about children who know from three or four years old that they are attracted to the same sex—or, for that matter, to another sex. A Foucauldian approach would argue that their recognition of themselves *as* homosexuals is the act of discourse that creates them *as* homosexual subjects.

Fair enough. But we are still left with some kind of core *identificatory structure*—let's not call it a Self, and let's definitely not call it "innate"—on which discourse acts. Behavioral psychologist B. F. Skinner famously boasted, "Give me a child, and I'll shape him into anything." But he couldn't make a gay child straight, or a transsexed child cisgender, or vice versa.

If there *is* any biological basis to the Self, it seems certain that the body, its erotic pleasures and sexuality are part of it. As Henry Rubin (following Merleau-Ponty) has noted, this phenomenological sense of body is fundamental to our subjectivity, a Heideggerian sense of *this* self in *this* world. Even when "the psychical representation of the body as it is for the subject [does] not correspond directly with the physical body."[33]

To look at one's body at age three or four or five, when ego, intellect, and ability articulate are all far from mature, and nonetheless refute the world's entire discursive machinery—including both the formal, top-down concrete powers of naming, sexing, identificatory documents, and the weight of school, medical, and religious systems, as well as the informal, diffuse, Foucauldian bottom-up powers of family and peer interactions—by declaring, "This is not how I should be. I have no proof. I have no experience of any other body. And I don't even have a name for it. But part of me knows better and knows how it should be."

This, by any measure, is a pretty astounding accomplishment. So many interesting questions arise from this, prime among them, how? How are trans children able to resist the full weight of the enormous discursive powers arrayed against them along with the evidence of their own flesh?

What does it mean to recognize one's identification with things that are feminine or masculine prior to fully internalizing or understanding the accompanying discursive positions of Man or Woman?

How are children able to imagine themselves with organs to which they have yet to be exposed?

What does their ability to do so tell us about the limits of social constructionism and postmodernism in explicating gender identity and gendered embodiment generally, and transsexual subjects specifically?

Why does a significant minority of trans children (like me) find that moment of refutation or self-recognition only when they are well into adulthood?

Queer theory, with its skepticism of selves and subjectivity, is unable to provide us with much information or direction here. And trans theory, which tends to answer to questions about gender identity by turning to biological essentialism, is hardly more informative and scarcely more satisfying.

Yet, I take such questions as at the very heart of trans studies engagement with transsexed subjects.

Oppression or Enlightenment?

We are still living the split between accounts
of the self and accounts of the subject.[34]

—HEATHER LOVE ("QUEER METHOD AND THE
POSTWAR HISTORY OF SEXUALITY STUDIES")

Once such a young person begins to recognize themselves *as*
transgender, and their feelings as evidence that they are really are a
girl or a boy, the queer theory/Foucauldian model might consider this
evidence of and a submission to discursive construction. But it can
also be understood as a kind of empowerment.

As B. George and Stacey Goguen argue in their paper,
"Hermeneutical Backlash: Trans Youth Panics as Epistemic Injustice,"
a lack of knowledge or "hermeneutical lacunae," which renders an
important part of one's experience unintelligible to one's own self,
can be understood as a kind of oppression itself. This is connected to
ethnographer Elfreda Chapman's concept of "information poverty"
in which marginalized groups suffer from barriers to accessing
knowledge that would improve their well-being.[35,36] And the process
of an abject individual locating themselves within the discourse can
also be alleviating, a type of *hermeneutical liberation.*[37]

I didn't have a name for what I was experiencing until I stumbled
across Harry Benjamin's landmark paperback, *The Transsexual
Phenomenon.* Even then—since neither I nor anyone in Cleveland's large
gay community had ever met anyone transsexual—I considered the idea
that I might be one so implausible that the book sat on my bookshelf for
a year. (In fact, I still consider it ridiculously implausible today.)

A late bloomer trans-wise, I had one of those quintessential "lightbulb" experiences around age twenty-six. Philosopher Miranda Fricker calls those abrupt "*Aha!*" moments of sudden recognition, which compel a "reinterpretation of a whole area of experience," *hermeneutical breakthrough*.[38,39] And indeed, beyond informing me that there was a name for what I experiencing, it finally enabled me to make some sense of my own tangled, tormented, and perpetually frustrating sexual history.

For me, this included the *erotic injustice* of being unable to make my sources of desire, arousal, and pleasure match the practices available to the body I'd been living in for over two decades. As Billy Huff asks, since "the current conceptual frame for being trans "limits our access to livable lives that include sexual pleasure [w]hat, then, might comprise erotic justice for trans subjects?"[40]

Perhaps because of his skepticism toward the Self, Foucault's idea of discipline could not and does not address the hermeneutic injustices inflicted on subjects, preventing them from seeing or understanding themselves. As with other forms of discursive violence, these kinds of harm are capillary, diffuse, impersonal, and gradual. It is the harm of accumulated disconfirmation and negation, lacking a single specific agent, event, or location but showing up as a gap in one's knowledge of and ability to recognize one's self or one's body and the discomfort that causes.

As Moria Peréz has explained, "[D]espite its magnitude and persistence, epistemic violence continues to be relatively marginal in the Humanities and Social Sciences, which—except for some perspectives focused on racial, colonial/postcolonial, or gender issues—have been reluctant to consider the epistemic realm as a specific site of violence."[41]

Queer theory and trans theory have been similarly reluctant. The former views any subject position with suspicion, even supposedly liberatory ones. And the latter has largely focused on the politics of trans existence *after* the moment of recognition and coming out. Was it my moment of self-recognition when I finally gained a better understanding of the things I was experiencing, my dysphoria, and how I might remedy it in a typically Foucauldian moment of discursive surrender, which only *felt* liberatory but still unintentional reiterated the very terms of my construction? Or was it a Frickerian moment of epistemic liberation, in which I was finally able to undo the hermeneutic and erotic injustice done to me by a discourse which had rendered my self and my experience unintelligible, including my finally understanding how I wanted to have sex, and how the body I had might be unable to accomplish the things that I wanted it to do?

As much as I treasure the intellectual fertility of postmodernism's *paranoid style* with its suspicion of discourse's perpetual power to smuggle itself in experience camouflaged as liberatory, here it seems Fricker's argument is the more compelling.

At the very least, as a sexual being, I would much prefer the oppression of being burdened with that discursive self-knowledge, the insights it allowed, and the post-op pleasures I have been finally able to enjoy, than the "bliss" of continued ignorance of all this.

The fact that such questions have no obvious solution shows the limits of queer theory in explicating the complex effects discourse for abjected subjects. It also shows how postmodernism is unable to engage with any form of hermeneutic insight that provides a sense of self-recognition, relief, and empowerment, that are immune from being recategorized as a discursive surrender. Ignorance is simply not always bliss—and it is certainly not pleasure.

An Intricate and Little-Studied Dance

Gayle Salamon tries to resolve the apparent nature versus nurture conflict by asserting that our "very feelings of embodiment, that seem to be the most personal, most individual, and most immune," are in fact still constructed, and it is only by examining this constructedness that we can find "a way to understand how felt sense arises."

Yet I'm unsure how we apply this to the gendered experience of children like me, who—if they are certainly no longer on *tabula rasa*— are the closest thing we have to it to see if our theories hold water. Or to reuse *Gender Trouble*'s analogy again, children may no longer be perfectly "raw," but they are certainly still a long way from being "cooked."[42] In any case, I think it may put us back in *Heads-I-win/Tails-you-lose* situation, where all moves inevitably lead back to constructedness.

Belief in the biological or neurological predicate cited by theorists like Lane, Prosser, and Serano is also the only way I can make sense of Straayer's data on trans men's experiences of their missing phantom penises from early childhood.[43] Perhaps such experiences do not seem dispositive to many readers, but they certainly take the wind out of any social constructionist sails for me.

Similarly, even after I learned about masturbation around age ten or so, while I could orgasm with an *outie*, I couldn't make it psychologically interesting or emotionally satisfying. The sensations were there, but I couldn't eroticize having an *outie* or imagine anything

I wanted to do with it or have done *to* it. It is hard to me to understand this as in the produce of discourse.

When I finally did have my long-delayed first intercourse using a penis with another woman, my initial excitement ebbed immediately upon insertion. It instantly gave way to disappointment, and then to boredom. I'm here reminded of Henry Rubin's plaintive questions, "What does it feel like to penetrate someone, to be inside another body? To ejaculate on or in someone?"[44] He was tormented by not knowing: I was becoming tormented by knowing, and not liking the answer. Although my partner seemed to be enjoying herself enough, I couldn't understand the point of the exercise and—somewhat relieved when it was finally over—I immediately resolved never to do it again.

But I *did* do it again; many times.

I quickly learned I could enjoy sex by displacing awareness of myself and instead imagining I was the woman I was with. I would ignore what my own body was doing and feeling to focus instead on how sexy it must be for her. Obviously I have no idea how it was for them or what they were feeling—I was just generating a sense of what I thought I might experience in their position and/or body.

Doing this was both arousing and highly unsatisfying, but it was the only way sex worked for me at all. I assumed that all men wanted to have sex with women because they wanted to *be* women. It was not until I had a very earnest talk with a penis-bearing male friend in my thirties that I realized this was not the case. I looked at him for a long moment and said, "Wait a minute: you *enjoy* having a penis and what you do with it." He smiled at me gently as if I was crazy, and answered that he *did*, very much so. I know it sounds like I must be stupid, but this actually came as revelation.

Perhaps my experience illustrates some small way the intricate and little-studied dance among arousal, pleasure, and embodied subjectively, and how body schema, sensation, and eroticism are inextricably connected. We don't just need nerve endings that feel good, we need nerve endings in specific configurations that do very specific things. Just because a sensation or configuration produces physical pleasure or even orgasm does not mean that it's erotic or sexually satisfying. It is possible to be physically aroused but not psychologically aroused.[45] Trans desire and arousal are as integral to sexual pleasure as any specific physical sensation.

Erotic Structuralism

In "When Selves Have Sex," Bettcher terms this phenomenon *erotic structuralism*.[46] Sexual attraction and fulfillment are complex processes which have an internal structure that encompasses the eroticized Other, eroticized self, and the interplay between the gendered self and the gendered other. Sexuality is bidirectional: we eroticize not only the other subject but also ourselves as desiring subject. As the old saw goes, the body's biggest sex organ is the brain. For Bettcher, the meaning of body parts and their acts is not a ciscentric given, but is actively created.

For instance, as brave and arresting as Rose's reframing of his vagina is, while contesting the requirement that sex be gendered ("pleasure is pleasure"), it also tends to gender both organs and their pleasures, showing just how closely arousal and sexuality are structurally intertwined.

Questions for trans studies abound. Erotic structuralism would seem to be a good foundation for reconceptualizing trans sexuality and the challenges of the experiencing pleasure in an unconfigured or reconfigured body, yet there is little published about either so far. Another question would be how one integrates into consciousness, into one's body image, into one's phenomenological experience of the body, and finally into the complex intimacy of sexual intercourse organs and new body parts with which one has no prior lived experience, and which may only recently have been (or still are) under construction.

Since surgery, I have always found that I need pretty specific sort of stimulation, and I am reminded here of one early lover who used to affectionately joke that my genitals should come with their own "Users' Manual." I have sometimes felt the same.

Howitt talks about trans sexuality as involving "assemblages," in which many trans people assemble—with surgery, hormones, naming, sexual acts, toys and appliances (binders, vibrators, dildos, etc.), and so on—exactly what they need to achieve pleasure and affirming erotic embodiment.[47]

Especially for those changing our genitalia, this is bound to change how we are able to get aroused, what we feel, how we want to be pleasured, and how we come in ways that are novel and perhaps even intricate. But only a tiny handful of studies have ever examined this and much more attention is needed to begin really understanding it.

All major surgeries are an insult to mind and body, especially this particular surgery in this particular place: among the body's most delicate and vascular, full of the special nerves that produce pleasure. It is a journey that many trans women (and men) have taken, from that trauma to integrating this new *pleasurable and corrective wound* and its strange sensations into consciousness and eroticism and thence into intimacy.

How is this possible? What are the main stages in this journey, and what are its main obstacles? How does one relearn to orgasm (or not) with this new configuration of flesh and nerve? What kind of phenomenological experience does this enable (or inhibit) during sex? What are the complexities of this new configuration, and how does it function sexually—and where it doesn't, what are its limitations?

Whatever the answers to questions like these, exploring them holds the promise of unique insights into the phenomenological consciousness of sexuality for which trans scholars (and perhaps also disability theorists, who often wrestle with similar issues) would seem to be uniquely qualified.

"Sweaty Concepts"

I grew up in the 1960s under a rage-aholic macho father who was psychologically and sometimes even physically abusive, and who despised any signs of weakness in his eldest (gay) son and in his younger (transsexed) one. And this helped inspired in me a deep fear and loathing for anything to do with vulnerability or softness.

"Inspired" is the right word, since no one actually told me to submerge and scorn these feelings—or ever had to. Even as a child, I understood the demand characteristics of the environment around me and what I had to do to survive in it. I sensed instinctively, as children do, that hiding who I was at all times was to be a primary necessity.

Unfortunately, children tend to be highly transparent: they don't know how to hide feelings, and they are aware that they are fully exposed to the adult gaze. Terrified that being aware of any feminine feelings in myself (let alone displaying them) would be instantly visible to him, I suppressed this side of myself completely, imagining myself and my body as masculine, aggressive, and butch as possible.

This was a joke of course. Riff, the macho, *uber*-buff leader of the Jets from *West Side Story* was my template. I failed utterly. Girls hated me because I always seemed to be yearning after them in a way that clearly wasn't hetero-romantic, and boys hated me because they suspected I was some sort of crypto-fag. They knew they were supposed to beat me up, and I knew they were too: we could just never agree on terms since I was a sports nut and pathetically, obviously attracted to girls.

Later, as an adult, I had become homophobic not in the sense that I abjured homosexuals or effeminacy in men—quite the contrary. But I instinctively loathed anything of it in myself. Whenever it raised its head, a homophobic Committee in my head would instantly convene and begin screaming at me how shameful and *faggy* I must look to others.

Sara Ahmed talks about such experiences as "sweaty concepts"— the difficulty and work of inhabiting a body not at home in a world and of having an experience of that body that is continually challenging and difficult. But rather than avoiding the labor, one keeps trying. And I tried—a lot.[48]

What an enormous cosmic jest, then, that while traditional feminine vulnerability filled me with disgust, it turned out to be a core facet of my gender and sexuality, whose suppression left me constantly depressed and dissociated.

Alas, transition and surgery were physical processes which did little to diminish this. Even during the years that I pursued my transition as a full-time job in itself, I resisted any sort of emotional transition. I would change my body, but not my gender expression.

In the late 1970s, I was probably the most butch transsexual woman anyone had ever seen. At trans conferences, I stuck out like a sore thumb among the crossdressers and other transsexual women.

By the 1980s, this sometimes earned me street cred from some trans folks for "being radical," or "queering gender." But I was a fake. Underneath my carefully curated androgyny lurked enormous, internalized disgust with anything soft or feminine in myself. Crossdressers would sometimes compliment me for my "bravery," but I would look at them in their dresses and makeup, ashamed and envious, aware that even as I allowed them to continue thinking that *I* was brave by *refusing to pass* and being *genderqueer*, they were the ones who really had the courage to be authentically themselves, embracing a femininity and a vulnerability I that I still could not bring myself to own.

Even when I worked on Wall Street and had to dress up *en femme*, I bought expensive power suits to go to work. My partner asked me once why I never wore dresses. When I pointed to my business wardrobe, she replied, "Those aren't dresses, they're armor," And she was right; I was still hiding myself in plain sight.

It wasn't clothing, hair, or makeup thing per se that was the issue—I was and am still pretty androgenous presenting—but how I allowed myself to experience my self and my body. When I allowed myself to *feel* my gender and my body, it still *felt* like such a public statement that it was like morphing into a walking personals ad that read: "Hi, we don't know each other but I have breasts and a vagina, I enjoy piña coladas and gettin' caught in the rain, and having a woman fuck me." In other words, decades of suppression mean being mean made me feel not just *authentic* or *present*, but *exposed*. So, I instinctively shut it down immediately, which left me depressed and numb.

Surviving (Re)Embodiment

It was about two months after my own surgery when, for the first time, I finally felt a woman moving inside me. I immediately knew that something big had changed. I wrote out a rigorous training schedule, purchased a Hitachi Magic Wand, and *viola!*—first post-op orgasm.

My doctor had told me that my vagina wouldn't lubricate, but in fact it did, just not on command, more like at completely random moments on some schedule I could never comprehend. I have begged my cisgender wife to teach me how hers does it at the right time, but she has so far refused (I suspect this is yet another way cis women keep us abjected).

GAS is often presented publicly as a *generative* surgery that creates something new, or else a reductive one, that *removes* something. But for us, it's merely a *reconstructive* one, which returns to us something we already had. Although Chu was right that such surgeries don't make us happy, they do provide important prerequisites for its possible emergence. Certainly for me, it was like a door finally opening.[49]

Alas, for four decades, I was unable to walk through it.

Having finally achieved the mental relief of a more feminine body in the form of breasts and a vagina, I promptly went about ignoring them all as much as possible, just as I had learned to ignore my penis and boy-body, if with infinitely less dysphoria.

While I had the organs I wanted for the body I wanted, I was unable to stay present for whatever sense of embodiment they made possible and whatever pleasures they had at last enabled.

Having a penis, while distinctly foreign and unpleasant, also felt distressingly invulnerable during sex. I say *distressing* because it was precisely the vulnerability that I found erotic—the idea of being vulnerable to another's touch in the most intimate way through penetration. I was in pursuit of exactly the semantic interpretation of my vagina that writer/poet Jody Rose was trying to confound with his. And unlike Chu, as I contemplated my own surgery, it occurred to me that fucking might finally be fun.

I had even, sometime before my surgery was scheduled, visited a gay male sex club just to make sure that real, live anal sex was really not the thing I was missing.

It was not. Yet another pleasant sneeze, but no cigar.

The most remarkable thing for me was that the place was overflowing with macho guys trying to out-butch each other as *more-top-than-you*, which left me the only self-identified bottom around and the main object of everyone's attention. Had that been erotic to me, I would have been in heaven, but it was all wasted on me.

Now that I was finally able to experience sex with the body and acts of my desires, I still found myself detaching and dissociating, going off someplace where I still felt invulnerable and in control. Mentally, I couldn't stop the cycle of finding enjoyment largely through safely fantasizing what my partner's body must be feeling while ignoring my own. This left me with less dysphoria but only slightly better *sneezes*. I could finally be fucked, but I couldn't be present for it.

Fear and Loathing at 5 A.M.

My own long path back to beginning to survive embodiment during sex had come in roughly three stages: Self-Hate, Fear, and Aesthetics.

I was a distance runner at the time, and I decided to dedicate my two-hour 5:00 a.m. runs to finally facing my demons. And it was during those long, empty, early mornings alone in the dark that every poisonous hypermasculine attitude I'd ever internalized finally came to the surface, again and again.

I was disgusted with myself and filled with self-loathing both for vulnerability and with the idea that I enjoyed this sexually. The vile epithets I yelled at myself mentally (and sometimes out loud around the National Mall's empty boulevards) sometimes shocked even me. I knew almost everyone carried some unrecognized self-hate inside, but I found I'd been sitting on this vast, underground reservoir which now slowly had to be drained like some enormous, poisonous abscess.

Next came Fear.

Being repeatedly terrorized and psychologically violated had taught me not to show or even acknowledge being a body, having a body, being in my body, or letting others see who I was through my body. All this felt immensely unsafe, dangerous and filled me with a reflexive terror.

I learned that reflexively visualizing myself through that masculine, boy-type body meant I would act appropriately in ways that would keep me safe around cisgender people, which meant my father and everyone else. When any other way of experience my body came to mind, any other feminized sort of body schema or feeling, I instinctively remobilized this "cisgender gaze," revisualizing my body as the cisgender Other saw it.

Having once been terrorized by my father, I was now terrorizing myself. Just as Foucault's panoptical *disciplinary power* perfectly predicted. Having internalized cisgender social norms, I had begun imposing them on myself even when alone.

Foucault had enumerated three key elements for *discipline*: permanent and hierarchical observation, normalizing judgment, and self-examination. I had all three in spades.[50]

The cisgender gaze perfectly fits this idea of discipline. It is hierarchical and omnipresent—because cis people are everywhere observing the gender nonconforming body which is always hyper-visible. It imposes a normalizing judgment—because genderqueer bodies are always being measured and judged according to how well the approximate cisgender genders. And it enforces self-examination—through a constant cycle of negative feedback, ridicule, and fear. It is one of the ironies of transgender life that the greatest compliment a cisgender person can grant is that they *never could have guessed* that we were trans because *we look just like them*. Because to look transgender is always a kind of failure.

(Decades ago, I let myself be filmed for a German documentary on the Transexual Menace, and just as the tape started rolling, I pointed at something with "broken wrist." I knew the moment I did it, it was a mistake. Sure enough, that stupid gesture was the opening shot. You could read invisible chyrons: *Look, look! a "trannie" doing something Just Like a Real Woman!*)

The point of disciplinary power is that it is not something done to us, but something we learn to do to ourselves. For instance, how many of us, before bottom surgery, examine pictures of the surgeon's work in order to compare it to cisgender bodies? And afterward, how many compare the results to cisgenitals to judge our procedure's success? How many of us are complimented or at least quietly pleased when we *pass* or silently bummed when we don't. As philosopher Sally Haslinger explains, "Under surveillance, we do [gender] to ourselves, voluntarily."

Internalized Gazes

Laura Mulvey theorized about women who internalize "the male gaze," but I found her description of it very closely tracked my own experience of the cisgender gaze. Here's my paraphrase:[51]

In a world ordered by power imbalance . . . looking has been split between active/cisgender and passive/transgender. The determining cisgender gaze projects its fantasy on to the gendered trans feminine form which is styled accordingly. In their traditional exhibitionist role, trans people are simultaneously looked at and displayed, with their appearance coded for strong visual impact and connoting to-be-looked-at-ness.

I had all the symptoms that studies show cis women develop from internalizing the "male gaze": consistent anxiety, increased surveillance, self-objectification, and an inability to stay in my body and be present for sex.

All this works as it is an effective defense mechanism that keeps fear at bay and helps me feel *safe* by reining in and shutting down my feelings, and substituting someone else's vision of me for my own. In fact, I doubt I would have survived my childhood—especially my father and the bullies at school—if I had stayed present in my body for it and not successfully internalized the cisgender gaze.

As K. J. Cerankowski writes in his shattering book-*cum*-memoir, *Suture: Trauma and Trans Becoming*, "Much of my life has been spent either trying to disappear or to become someone else. Becoming someone or something else is, I suppose, its own kind of disappearance."[52]

My disciplinary internalization of the cisgender gaze was essentially a trauma reaction, it was a corrosive self re-traumatization I'd adopted as protection. But while this kept me safe, it made me crazy and miserable. And it came with nasty little side effects, such as regular nightmares with nightsweats, disordered eating, and the exhaustion of constant hypervigilance. The fact is, unless you can hold yourself with gentleness and acceptance, you can never find peace—which is difficult for trans people because too few of us still have a lot of experience of being treated with gentleness and acceptance.

My depersonalization was especially fierce. As Jules Gill-Peterson observes, "Dissociation feels much more pregnant with possibility, something like a trans method."[53] I would frequently find myself unexpectedly dissolving into tears when home alone, without the slightest idea what emotion I was feeling. I would go to the bathroom to look in the mirror, examining my wet, contorted face for clues of my emotions.

There were entire days, actually entire decades, through which I sleepwalked. I was a person of privilege—young, white, educated, post-op, employed—and by any external measure enjoying a pretty good life. But when you don't have yourself, "everything" is also another kind of "nothing," because everything is happening to someone else.

A pre-op transsexual body might have been painful place to live, but since it wasn't really mine anyway, it had also been a dandy place to hide out from my feelings and my life. I thought all this would change with transition and surgery, but instead it barely budged. I still found living in a transsexed body so absurd that I still refused to believe in it. As agender writer Tyler Ford puts it, "I always felt like a walking brain: living in my head, while everyone around me seemed to have some innate understanding of their bodies."⁵⁴ I lived in my head as much as possible—which, for a systems programmer with ADD, was practically a job requirement.

The events of my life continued to feel like they were happening under glass as I waited obstinately, resentfully, fruitlessly for "real life" to show up and start. As John Lennon told us, *life is what happens while you're waiting for something else.* And it's taken and still takes a lot of patient work to interrupt that reflexive trauma cycle and become present. Some days are good; others aren't.

I'm often puzzled over why this has been so difficult. Simply disrupting a toxic mental cycle which kept recapitulating the same painful sense of gender and the same painfully gendered bodily schema in my head should have been easy. My theoretical beliefs told me that this gendered experience should have been a *do*-ing, not a *be*-ing: unstable, always in danger of failing. I even *wanted* it to fail. Instead, it might as well have been welded in place.

Every time I would get beneath it and touch anything that felt more *me*, it would trigger an intense trauma reaction: I'd feel disoriented, weepy, afraid of losing control combined with that awful sense of impending doom, and I'd start to develop a nasty tension headache— basically all classic symptoms of a moderate anxiety attack.

If my experience is any guide, Butlerian notions of gender and their avoidance of its psychic aspects mean they are unable to account for the unexpected stability of many kinds of gendered experiences like this.

Over time, I have come to believe that agreeing with the cisgender gaze about what my body *means* or *is* or *looks like* is not so important. I don't think that the cis gaze has any monopoly on interpreting my body. How others see me may or not be ontologically *out there*, but my feelings about my body certainly are.

As for my disordered eating, which I've had continuously since about age six, I suspect that addictions may be another facet of transgender embodiment about which we don't talk much but I suspect may be a quiet epidemic. Especially around food, since it's the first substance we can abuse as children, and so many of us are gender-abused as children. As Susie Orbach explained long ago in her book, *Fat Is a Feminist Issue*, overeating helped me escape, suppress my feelings, to enjoy at least one bodily pleasure that was under my control.[55] And the extra layer of body fat along with that sense of being overly full felt like protection, a small bit of armor between me and the disciplinary gaze.

Whenever I felt skinny or my stomach empty, I would feel more vulnerable and thus more feminine and sexy—which quickly became intolerable. So I overate daily, and then dieted and exercised it off constantly. It was a six-decade struggle, an endless and pointless cycle. Unsurprisingly, I do find that as my dysphoria and disassociate decrease, and my sense of embodiment improves, my need to overeat diminishes.

Again, I now recognize that this is often how many people deal with trauma, and the nightmares, addictive behaviors, anhedonia, and body disassociation, which are all among the classic symptoms of PTSD. I have now interviewed or spoken with trans people from a variety of countries, races, and ethnicities who report having similar experiences. As one trans male scholar confided to me, "I think this is why I do 'shrooms."[56,57] Although I have no data other than my own experience and talks with others, I suspect that—like substance abuse—subacute chronic PTSD stalks the trans community like a silent epidemic that is all around but nowhere spoken of. And until we break that silence, we cannot begin to heal it.

Aesthetic Imperialism

After Self-Hate and Fear came stagethree: Aesthetics.

As Binnie writes in *Nevada*, "The moment her pants come off, she stops being in her body, and when she's off in the clouds desperately trying to make an emergency peace with her own junk."[58] And indeed, as soon as I found myself at the end of a date, taking my pants off for a longed-for and long-sought moment of lesbian intimacy, I found myself desperately trying to make emergency peace with my own *junk*, even though I finally had *the junk of my desires*. For me, only part of the challenges of transsexed embodiment could be resolved by medication and scalpels. Growing up, my body had never been a safe place to be, and that was something no surgeon could fix.

The fact that I had cisgender lovers who were fine with my genitals, even aroused by them, made no difference. I had absorbed the conviction that the crucial posture to have toward my new genitals, as with the rest of my body, was one of judgment, rather affirmation or (god forbid!) enjoyment.

So even when I felt good, I would scan my body or check a mirror to see how I might look to the cis-Other. What I was really checking was that internalized, highly gendered, body schema I had built up over years for how I thought cisgender people saw me.

The problem is, I had no trans-centric aesthetic by which to compare it, or even to shift to, because we don't have one. Trans theory has seldom engaged with this problem (except in its negative impacts on passing, etc.). Perhaps in a time of such political peril, its seems frivolous. By taking aesthetics as a given, our dominant notions of femininity and masculinity default to those of the cis-Other—including many of our personal standards for successful transition, hormonal effects, surgical outcomes, and so on.

What might the femininity and masculinity many of us seek mean, if they were totally unmoored from the binary sex of the cisgender body? Ideals that most of us can only approximate, some of us can't approximate at all, some of us don't even want to, and others want to but for various reasons (health, money, etc.) have bodies that feel *unfinished*. What would a specifically transgender aesthetic of femininity and masculinity (or even genderqueerness) for all such bodies look like?

This is not a rhetorical question. Abjected communities that fail to critique their own aesthetics or treat them as natural facts are often doomed to internalize those used to oppress them. Although enormous attention has been invested in analyzing *gender, gender identity*, and the *gender system*, gender expressions is only not deconstructed, but—other than drag—understood as topic worthy of little critical attention.

This has left trans studies lacking any theory of what a trans-centric aesthetic might be or how it might offer an alternative set of terms for what bodies can and should look like, or a deeper critique of the aesthetics of gendered dimorphism. Simply saying that as a community, we embrace a multiplicity of bodies and gender expressions is not a substitute for an analysis of aesthetics of erotic attraction or sexual beauty that appear to be tethered (as nonbinary writer R. E. Wallace complained earlier) to binary sexual dimorphism.

And what is the entire cisgender aesthetic of masculinity and femininity with its idolization of *large breasts on soft-faced, hairless women and musculature on stubbly men with chiseled jaws* except the fetishization of binary dimorphism?

To paraphrase Kate Millett's famous complaint about the patriarchy, the aesthetic of cisgender binary dimorphism is so universal that it's hard to imagine an alternative to which it might be contrasted and thus critiqued. It presents itself and is perceived as natural and therefore inevitable. To have a trans body and post-op genitalia that are "successful" is to have those that fit as closely as possible the prevailing cisgender aesthetic, with all alternatives permanently foreclosed—what Lugones might understand as a raced and gendered colonization of the trans body.[59]

Cis-aesthetics operate as visual hegemony: a ritualized, daily, epistemic violence for those of us who don't fit into it very well that reinforces our sense of failure and gendered inferiority. It is a kind of *aesthetic imperialism.*

While race and gender are different, if intersecting, factors, the "Black Is Beautiful" movement provides one extraordinary example of how an abjected community critiqued, reinterpreted, and inaugurated its own aesthetic ideals in the face of overwhelming aesthetic imperialism. I sometimes feel if all that *retooling* and *recoding* of the transgender body may not be the seeds of a trans-centric aesthetic.

In any case, cisgender people aren't the only game in town; they're just one game in one town.

The task of theorizing and constructing such an aesthetic, if it is undertaken one day, will be deeply complicated by the coming schism in the transgender community, which is going to increasingly split cleanly in many between those who have had early access to blockers, hormone therapy, and surgery and those who haven't. As they slowly become a majority in many places, the former—who will also skew markedly younger—are likely to have lifetime arcs, political priorities, and aesthetic sensibilities about their bodies' secondary sexual characteristics.

Regardless, when it comes to primary sexual characteristics, I suspect all of us may risk still ending up trapped in a web of cisgender aesthetic expectations and standards. As Plemons explains in his remarkable analysis of the politics of the transmasculine penis, "It Is As It Does," our aesthetic vision of bodies is "the product of disciplined ways of seeing . . . [I]deas about what constitutes the 'natural' body are not simply reflections of objective facts, but are created in situated practice."[60]

Thus, "ideas about what the body *does* (or does not do) significantly shape what we think the body *is*." *And* the aesthetics of how it should look.

In fact, Plemons specifically connects these situated aesthetics to knowledge about how the "natural body" is supposed to appear. And this is strongly heavily influenced by raced, classed, and colonial ways of seeing. Which is to say, we allow cisgender reproductive function to define the aesthetics of genitals in much the same ways we allow its cisgender dimorphism to define our ideas of beauty.

Within such constraints, how could the transgender body appear as anything other than an aesthetic failure? A site for shame and self-consciousness?

Internal Reality Enforcement

As Hil Malatino's essay "Future Fatigue" reminds us, like Chu, that path after transition and affirming care is not always a smooth one, but can leave us with "bad feelings that transition doesn't, can't possibly, eliminate."[61] As important as care of the body is, part of transition will always been an *inside job*.

If my intense aesthetic shame and self-judgment had cisgender fingerprints all over it, it was impossible to blame cisworld entirely for it, because I had long ago begun inflicting it on myself in ways that had become inseparable from my sense of my body.

I recall an essay by a trans man who had built himself into a strong, muscular bodybuilder. But after competing on stage, showing off his massive physique, he still heard this little voice in his head taunting him, "You're still just a little girl." That little voices for him is the aesthetic Committee that meets hourly in my head, and it was saying the same things, just in reverse.

My issue wasn't only external reality enforcement, but an internal one, too. The "contest of interpretations" that was now hurting me the most wasn't between cisgender people and me, it was between me and me—and yet somehow I kept losing.

I know such observations cut against the grain of trans critical theory, which locates trans oppression almost entirely with cissociety. But I believe I have and do contribute to my own self-oppression in important ways. For instance, over time I noticed that the woman I unconsciously tended to pick out to critique my own (lack of) femininity were exemplars of the kind of traditional slender, white Eurocentric attractiveness that would have been completely at home among Austin Power's Fembots. It was crazy—like pre-programming myself for shame and self-rejection.

Such inner contests are a key part of why the external misgendering and disconfirmations were so painful: they resonated with and amplified something in me.

I hear echoes of this in Chu's observation that she is highly uncomfortable and self-conscious about her hands—"I now feel very strongly about the length of my index fingers." While only she knows her own experience, it seems unlikely that any of us has felt "trapped in the wrong fingers," or that cisworld has relentlessly surveilled and shame us about our finger length.

In my case, I internalized a similar kind of shame—a repetition of the external traumatization which I enacted on myself in private. Healthy shame is where we do something wrong, feel bad, and change. But toxic shame is characterized by deep self-loathing over something we are that cannot be changed but which—like a drop of ink in a glass of water—colors everything.

In my books of interviews with trans people about addictive behaviors, they frequently used words to describe their early feelings about themselves as "a shame beyond shame," "a toxic shame about my body," "freak," "unlovable and worthless," "abomination," and "a broken monstrosity."[62]

Psychologist Gershen Kaufman writes that toxic shame is connected to "clusters of shame bound in images that are intensified by affect and interpretation," representational "snapshots" that we recycle endlessly—an internalization of our abjection by others.[63] Which is a pretty good description of what I was doing to myself with my own version of Chu's finger shame.

One example was my labia, which were created from my scrotal skin so that they still tended to relax or droop a bit when standing. So during sex with a (cis) lover, I made sure I was lying on my back. I would also make sure the lights were off to discourage close inspection. Even with long-time lovers I always wondered how they eroticized my vagina, yet I never asked any because I was afraid of the answer.

This is, I realize in retrospect, all kind of ridiculous. I had plenty of partners over the years, and none of them remarked about my labia or even seemed to notice them. At least, certainly none of them asked for their money back. But as with Chu and her index finger length, *I* was aware of it, and grew highly self-conscious and ashamed over it. Thus do cisnormative aesthetic ideals unconsciously morph over time into internalized transnormative ones and eventually into toxic shame.

On this and many other matters about my body, I'd unconsciously manufactured my own internal cis-centric critique and inflicted it on myself, importing this endless Gender Death Match into my head where it held daily, sometimes hourly, contests of interpretation—me against the Committee.

Clinging Like Vapor

It has helped that I no longer believe in any objective aesthetic reality to bodies, and that gendered meanings do not cling like vapor to the body parts to which we attach them, however compelling this illusion may be. I don't think it's possible to maintain that gender is constructed without also accepting that the highly dimorphic aesthetics of gendered bodies are as well, and its idolization of sexual dimorphism.

The fact is, male and female bodies aren't really that different. I doubt a Martian landing here for the first time would look at both bodies and yell out (in Martian of course), "Holy moly, these two things totally different!" I also doubt my Dachshund, *Churro*, who I suspect views all humans as vertically challenged, does either.

While there may indeed be individual limits to reinterpretation as Hale suggests—I certainly have run up against my own—theoretically I believe nearly infinite interpretations of the body's aesthetics are possible. Because, aesthetic regimes, despite seeming to be *really there* "on the far side of language" are highly contingent—as Plemons, Lugones, and so many others have pointed out. [64]

(As with everything, there appear to be some minor exceptions. For instance, some of facts of facial beauty seem to be at least in part a function of symmetry, in which features that are average of all others are perceived as attractive. It seems likely this has some biological basis—perhaps because of unconscious links between symmetry and health. But this also depends on what we're averaging—the average face changes across different time periods, races, ethnicities, and so on—so this appears to be contingent too.)

The existence of competing aesthetic interpretations of the body as well as the discontinuities and inconsistencies *within* aesthetics show that there is no singular body anywhere in evidence.

There is not one body, but many.

It is just that we privilege certain interpretations "the real" while dismissing others, as Chu does with her girlfriend's. If, as Butler said, gender is a repeated stylization of the body that congeals over time, I believe this repeated styling encompasses is not just our gender expression but also the gendered representations we build in our heads. Neither Butler nor queer theory have much to say about this body schema, because it involves internal states of the dreaded Self.

This schema is far from a specific and detailed snapshot. Instead, most of us carry around a general sense that we identify as our body which we mistake for an accurate representation. (You can test this by imagining your favorite actor and then looking at a photo. The schema you generated was probably very different and much less detailed.)

In terms of my own body, I wasn't just depressed about the naked body which I saw in the mirror, which I didn't really see it all that much. But scores of times each day, I did pull out that mental representation, what Merleau-Ponty called the *body consciousness*, I used it in my lifework. Except that, in my case, the lifework was to keep myself numb and protected. Thinking that because it was probably how most of the world saw me, which means most cisgender people, then it must be a real and accurate way of seeing my body.

But even the body in the mirror was, like the body I saw in my head, deeply formed and deformed by cisgender aesthetics. And interestingly, as I healed, they both changed over time—first the schema in my head and then the body I saw in the mirror.

Chu wrote, "When my girlfriend tells me I'm beautiful, I resent it. I've been outside. I know what beautiful looks like. Don't patronize me."[65] So, a description of her as "beautiful" is met with a dismissal as patronizing her, because she doesn't or can't see her body through her girlfriend's aesthetic lens. She fails to step outside her own, accepting it as a given, as *really there*. So, she does not interpret her girlfriend's comment as evidence of two competing aesthetics, but rather that her girlfriend must be seeing her body the same way but is only trying to be kind. She dismisses it as a valid alternative aesthetic understanding and reading of her body.

Chu's explanation for this is that she's *been outside* and thus she *knows what beautiful looks like*, is, I think, exactly wrong. I'm sure she's "been outside." But unless it was at Southern Comfort Conference, all she saw out there were the cisgender women who constantly surround us from birth. I sincerely doubt she has ever "been outside" of the cisgender bodily aesthetics by which feminine beauty is understood and constructed, much less the way they tend to be naturalized as defined solely by cis-feminine ideals, or even the way we as trans people are expected and encouraged to perform a kind of continuous corporeal comparison between our own gender features with others. As Malatino has written, do we ever know

> a moment when we are—transparently, in all our complexity, intuitively and deeply—known by those others we share space with? Where those others understand our bodyminds in precisely the ways in which we desire them to? Even if such moments are possible, or at least feel possible, that doesn't erase the prior years of consistent dissonance, misgendering, and misrecognition, nor does it easily transform the anxiety and fear that one cultivates as a product of living through such (routine, quotidian, incessant) moments.[66]

While I didn't resent lovers who told me I was attractive (and this wasn't a long line anyway), I *was* totally confounded by their attraction. And like Chu, I tended to dismiss their aesthetic appreciation instead of trying to learn from it, missing an important opportunity to get outside my own internalized transphobia to experience a different way of seeing my body. I recall one (cis)partner I met at Camp Trans of all places. When I told her I felt like a dork being so tall around all these shorter women, she told me she thought of me as a swan. It may be one of the nicest things anyone ever said about my body, and of course I dismissed it immediately as an incorrect way to see me.

Theorist Jean Baudrillard coined *transaesthetics* to refer to how the universality of everyday culture crosses boundaries, intermixes, and loses meaning. I propose trans studies might want to consider retasking this term to also refer to an alternative, trans-centric aesthetic of the transgender body.

No Original

What we see through the "arrogant eye" is an extraordinarily compelling illusion, but it is only that. No body is on the *far side of language*. As Chu's girlfriend and my own illustrate, there are many ways to interpret the trans body, not just one. I had no singular "other body" that all cis people saw. Instead there were a multiplicity of bodies that a multiplicity of people were seeing. To paraphrase Butler, the body we see ourselves having and the various bodies that others see us as having are all *copies for which there is no original.*[67]

Shilder describes the body image as "the picture of our own body which we form in our mind [and] the way it appears to ourselves."[68] But there is no one picture or one appearance to others. And the picture I'd formed in my mind was merely something I assumed that others saw and forced myself to "see" as by body schema whenever I became conscious or self-conscious of my body. Thus, as Henry Rubin declares, "The body image need not correspond with the physical body."[69] What is less obvious in this statement is that there was never a singular physical body to correspond *with*. There are many ways to read any physical body—it's just that we validate some, and disfavor others. As Chu and I did.

The notion that our body is "out there," that there must be one and only one way of understanding it that is *real*, so everyone is all seeing the same thing, may be a universal notion, but it is little more than a convenient social fiction, an artifact of cislogocentrism, an essentialization of the flesh that sustains and naturalizes its dominant reading of the body.

It is not only a product of the colonization of genderqueer bodies but also the very means by which that colonization is conducted. There is not one body but many.

Which one we see is highly contingent and the product of many factors:

Context changes perception. In many Asian nations, average height is several inches shorter than that in the United States and average breast size among women tends to be smaller. Yet when I went to Phnom Penh, I found Cambodian women didn't generally think of themselves as "short" or "small breasted"; they thought of Americans as "tall" and "large breasted." In a similar vein, I once had a chance to work out with a semi-pro women's basketball team, and as the runt on court, I reveled in the sudden and novel sense of being *petite*.

Age is also part of context. Most people see themselves younger than they actually look to others.[70] When I was younger, I thought old people looked impossibly old, wrinkled, and unattractive. But now that I'm one of them, I look pretty good. I find older women *hot*, and young women look impossibly, ridiculously smooth and unformed— please, I think I look about forty to everyone(!)

Standards change perception. Many readers will no doubt have skeptically read stories about models who look ridiculously beautiful to us, but can tick of an endless list of their "flaws"—imperfections invisible to almost anyone else. But the aesthetic standards internalized by those in an industry populated with impossible (traditional) beauty deform the perception of it. Similarly, it is now a well-known fact (and the subject of a multistate lawsuit against Meta) that Instagram causes distress in about a third of teenage girls because repeatedly viewing photoshopped and AI-produced bodies narrows and distorts their aesthetic standards.

Time period changes perception. George Reeves of the 1950s black-and-white *Superman* TV show had a jowly face, noticeably rounded tummy, no visible chest, and flabby arms. Christopher Reeve of the 1980s *Superman* movies had six-pack abs and a taut, muscular build. By the 2010s, Henry Cavill in the rebooted Superman movies was completely "shredded" like a professional bodybuilder. No doubt, audiences from each generation found their Superman a "natural" expression of ideal masculinity, and each would find the other's aesthetic sensibility incomprehensible.

Women's bodies have also gone through distinctly different aesthetic "styles" of feminine beauty, from the "classic" 1940s–1950s large-breasted, hourglass figures of Sophia Loren, Jane Russell, and Marilyn Monroe, to the 1960s and Twiggy's prepubescent anorexic ideal (which has recently reemerged on runways as "heroin chic"), to models and actors who show the lean, striated muscularity of the a professional personal trainer. Yet the ancient Greeks and the Europeans of the Renaissance saw the epitome of the feminine beauty aesthetic in curvy, rounded, *zaftig* fleshy bodies with high levels of adipose fat. Many subcultures in the United States today also prize this kind of feminine beauty.

Even women's body parts go through different styles, readings, and contexts. In feudal Japan, the nape of a woman's neck was highly eroticized, in part because it was the only exposed part of a geisha's body besides her face and hands. For the same reason, here in the United States around the turn of the last century (no, the one *before* that one), the sight of a woman's well-turned feminine ankle was eroticized, because it was also one of the few exposed areas of their bodies. Today, aside from ankle fetishists (*you* know who you are), ankles are generally aesthetically meaningless—a men's magazine focused on a "well-turned ankle" would be incomprehensible.[71] Erotic and gendered aesthetics tend to work with and on what is available to them.

Even awareness that there *is* a specific kind of feminine aesthetic appears to be discursively contingent. Jill Burke's book, *How to Be a Renaissance Woman*, documents how the adoption of the printing press combined with the reproduction of Renaissance painting in them presented many European women with the idea that there was a specific feminine ideal, in this case centered on pale, Eurocentric, curvy, apple-cheek and rosy-lipped bodies. Acting as the Instagram of its age, this began to define the expected feminine aesthetic of what was acceptable and expected, greatly accelerating the widespread adoption of cosmetics and other body modification practices.[72,73]

Culture changes perception. Exposing the female breast was "the norm in traditional cultures of North America, Africa, Australia and the Pacific Islands until the arrival of Christian missionaries . . . [and] in various Asian cultures before the Muslim expansion."[74] In many indigenous societies, the sight of female breasts is not considered indecent or immodest or even particularly erotic. Yet in the United States, publicly exposing the female breast can get you ogled, harassed, and jailed.

Like other Eurocentric societies, we find kissing—particularly, deep passionate kisses—highly erotic and intimate. But kissing is practiced in *less than half* of world's cultures, and many of those who don't find the practice disgusting, unsanitary, and aesthetically gross.[75]

And then there's that cherished staple of American cisgender manhood, the large penis, which one might assume would enjoy a pretty universal position as a symbol of manliness. Yet, as I've written elsewhere:

> The ancient Greeks . . . found small penises masculine and attractive. Large penises were considered animal-like, and they were often the butt (sorry) of public jokes. Men with big dicks learned to be ashamed of their genitals, and would "tuck" them, just like any sensible drag queen. A trans male friend who had recently returned from Greece told me how comfortable he'd felt in land where all the statues and pictures everywhere had small, manly dicks—just like his.[76]

Aesthetics and the readings of the body also shift within subaltern cultures. As Morgan Carpenter and others point out in their "Small Dick Energy" essay, in intersex/DSD culture, dicks and phalluses of different sizes are not stigmatized or disdained as unmanly or, for that matter, unfeminine.[77]

And while many people probably don't pay particular attention to beauty aesthetic of the asshole, many gay men do. "Anal rejuvenation" (*Repair. Restore. Rejuvenate!*) to create a more beautiful butthole is an increasingly popular procedure, which can even include such add-ons as bleaching and Botox.[78] And while most of us probably connect masculinity with things like muscles, strong cheekbones, and a taut six-pack, in gay "Bear Culture" masculinity is centered around things like being big, fat-positive, hairy, older, and sexually approachable.

Based on all this, we might want to extend Butler's formulation to say that gender is the repeated styling of the body within a strict regulatory frame that *is itself culturally and temporally contingent.* So hairiness, bigness, and strength don't *mean* masculine and smallness, softness, and curviness don't *mean* feminine, but turn out to be largely yet another facet of gender that congeals over time to produce the appearance of a natural substance.

The Un/Reality of Bodies

Cisgender gender aesthetics posits a threefold consonance between an observing and experiencing party: we see a subjects' body as having a particular gender expression; we understand that gender as being ontologically "there" and being expressed by that subject, and that the subject is phenomenologically experiencing their gender this way.

It's a compelling illusion and certainly how many people navigate the world. But I would argue that all of these are contingent, and there is no necessary connection between any of them. Since here are many aesthetics of masculinity and femininity circulating in different cultures at any time, there is no necessary consonance between how we read someone's body and how they experience them or what they "are." That young curvy, large-breasted blond may actually feel androgenous or manly. That tall, dark, muscular guy might be (probably is!) wearing women's underwear and feeling especially soft and feminine today.

This is one of the things that makes *thinking* gender so difficult: the bodies and genders that are so compelling aren't necessarily "out there" either ontologically for those of us who see them or how the person in that body experiences them.

With that said, I think many cisgender people do feel like their bodies are aesthetically perceived by the dominant culture. I don't know why this is, and like many trans people, I've never personally experienced it. It has always felt "natural" that there was a complete disconnect at all three levels: between how I felt, how my body looked to me, and how it looked to others.

When I first contemplated transition, I told myself I wanted to look like a cisgender woman looked. Then I realized that wasn't exactly accurate: it was more like I wanted to feel like a cisgender woman felt. But then I realized that wasn't accurate either. I have no idea how anyone feels. So what I really wanted was to feel the way I felt when I looked at some cisgender women's bodies and felt that familiar tug or resonance of recognition.

Perhaps this is some of what Salamon meant when she wrote that "[T]he body is available to the subject only through a complex set of mental representations . . . [which] shows that the body of which one supposedly has a 'felt sense' is not necessarily contiguous with the physical body as it is perceived from the outside."[79]

As Butler said of gender itself, I increasingly see gender aesthetics as a repeated stylization of the body that produces the illusion of a *natural* aesthetics of masculinity and femininity, *and* with it the illusion that people are gendered in the way that we see them.[80] Yet, as Lugones reminds us, how bodies are read is deeply entwined with the racist, ableist, and colonialist interpretations of gender that have often been inflicted on the colonized bodies over the strenuous objections of their occupants.

Thus, when someone insists on their interpretation, such as when I insist that you address me as "Ma'am" even though you see me as "really a guy," because gender is so strongly socially regulated, a clash of competing attempts at "realty reinforcement" ensues. (A somewhat less-loaded example might be when I insist that my seventeen-year-old daughter think of me as "cool.")

I'll See It When I Get Hot Over It

Among the main anchors of our sense of bodily gendered aesthetics is, of course, erotic attraction. We might again reformulate Butler's notion of gender once again as the "repeated stylization of the body the within a strict rigid regulatory *and erotic* frame that . . . produces the appearance of substance and forms objects of sexual and romantic attraction." Our sense of gender is inextricably intertwined with our sense of erotic attraction. It's a lot of what makes sex, sexy.

This is so obvious and well-known that it is surprising that it is almost never mentioned in queer or trans studies or even in feminism.

If you find hairy, muscular chests manly and hot (or for that matter a turn-off), it is much harder to read them or even conceive of reading them any other way. It not only tends to crowd out competing perceptions, but the erotic attraction you feel anchors and enhances your feeling that the masculinity you read is *really there* as a natural fact of the body.

This phenomenon also forms an important part of cisgender transphobia, although trans theory seldom mentions it. In "Evil Deceivers and Make Believers, On Transphobic Violence and the Politics of Illusion," Bettcher connects this to the hostility some cishet males feel upon having been "deceived" by trans women.[81] Surely this is part of it. But also "mannish" women like me are in some way asserting themselves publicly as feminine erotic objects. This is part of what enrages transphobic cishet bigots and arouses aesthetic confusion, discomfort, or even disgust when I am read as combining elements of both feminine appeal with masculinity/manhood. It is safe to say that if all trans women looked like Taylor Swift, Beyoncé, or Shakira, young men would probably be significantly less transphobic and cissociety a lot less hateful toward us.

For me, this animus worked on a kind of "sliding scale" with inverse costs and benefits. The more strongly I presented as feminine (dress, makeup, etc.), the more likely I was to *pass* as a woman, but also the more likely young cishet males were to feel affronted by my feminine display if they saw me as male.

Conversely, if I was presenting androgynously, I was less likely to *pass*, but bigoted guys were also less likely to be hostile toward me, since they did not read me as presenting myself as an object of feminine erotic attraction in the first place.

I want to be clear here that by "erotic attraction," I don't mean to imply actual arousal or romantic attraction. But for trans women, simply utilizing the aesthetics of the feminine gender and feminine gender expression is to mine the semiotics of arousal and attraction. As mentioned before, this includes dresses and blouses display the figure and flesh; eye and lip makeup make the face appear aroused with sexual interest, even the feminine postural, gestural, and vocal system—the classic one-legged stork pose, the broken wrist and tilted head, and the high-rising terminals at the end of both declarative and interrogative sentences—all of which communicate a feminine vulnerability.

And the right also leverages this confounding of gendered erotics and aesthetics against us. For years, I've tracked the images they use to try to stir up fear, loathing, and derision toward transgender women. Invariably, the image is of a markedly hirsute man with five o'clock shadow in a low-cut dress, long hair, and makeup. Even all the way back in 1995, Concerned Women of America's response to the first National Gender Lobby Day was a cartoon like this.[82] Today, they're still widely used (here's a more recent example: https://x.com/grandoldmemes/status/1817666334823518436). The synthesis of strong feminine signifiers with strong masculine signifiers is designed to produce disgust and disdain.

Nothing here is the slightest bit new or surprising. Everyone, cis and trans, knows it. And I expect many trans people have experienced one or another aspect of it. Trans studies just hadn't devoted much attention to it. But erotic aesthetics remain central to how cis people experience us as trans and how we experience ourselves.

Toxic Shame and Transnormativity

In my case, a kind of toxic shame—a repetition of the external traumatization which I enacted on myself in private.

Healthy shame is where we do something wrong, feel bad about it, and change it. But the toxic shame that Gershen Kaufman speaks of is characterized by a deep sense of self-loathing over something we are and which cannot be changed but recycles endlessly and—like a drop of ink in a glass of water—colors everything about us.

One example for me was related to my labia, which were created from my scrotal skin so that it still tended to relax or droop a bit when I was standing. So whenever a (cis) lover was around my naked body during sex, I made sure that I was lying on my back. It was something like the trans-femme equivalent of holding your stomach in to look thinner, or Chu's saying she would hide her fingers when holding hands with her girlfriend—but in my case it was also intertwined with my shame about the origins and aesthetics of my post-op genitals.

I would also make sure the lights were off or dim, to discourage close inspection because I could never be sure what a new lover's reaction would be to my vagina. Even with long-time lovers I always wondered if they eroticized my vagina, similarly to the way they would others, yet I never asked any of them because I was afraid of getting an answer I wouldn't like.

This is, I realize in retrospect, all kind of ridiculous. I had plenty of partners over the years, and none of *them* remarked about this or even seemed to notice it. (Certainly none of them asked for their money back.) But as with Chu and her index fingers, I *was aware of it* and grew highly self-conscious and ashamed of it. Thus do cisnormative aesthetic ideals unconsciously morph over time into internalized transnormative ones as well.

An Obligation of Abnormality

Most people have an unconscious somatic center of gravity, and this contributes to our sense of embodiment and the body *schema* we internalize for thinking about how we look. For me (as for most men), this had always been in my shoulders. But I found as I became willing to have hips and breasts, my mental center of balance shifted downward. As I shed some of this muscular tension, I also found myself feeling less dissociated and less dysphoric. I had always held my hips rigidly in place. But as I allowed myself to feel more embodied, my hips began to sometimes, ummm, move when I walked. (I want to be *very* clear here: they did *not* wiggle—I would *never* do that.)

This came and went, but there was generally a definite shift in my gait and carriage. And my shoulders, which were perpetually tight and up around my earlobes to shield me from The Blow That Is Always About to Fall, started to relax and lower as well. On a very basic level, posture was a way to take my body back and reown it.

Cis women's hips sway at least in part because of their pelvis, and probably, at least partly, because it increases attractiveness to het males.[83,84] But neither of these applied to me. So I wondered: Why was *I* doing it? Was I unconsciously imitating what I'd seen other women do? Or was it something innate but suppressed?

It was as if my behavior needed to be *authorized* in a way that my normal boy hip rigidity did not. So why did one require a *reason*, while the other *just was*? In *Read My Lips*, I described the trans body as a site of "constraint and authorization."[85] Thus, my manly stalking and hulking posture required no explanation, while my (hopefully fetching) hip sway, softened shoulders, and lengthened neckline did need one. They had to come forward and explain themselves. When I found myself doing anything femme, I was quickly sucked back into the Doom Loop in my head, where the Gender Police Committee had begun calling itself into emergency session.

I had to remind myself that the things my body does are not, or at least not, only citational performances or repeated stylizations. They're just things my body now does.

This leads directly to what I think of as the *obligation of abnormality* with which I think transsexuals are often saddled, not only in the cisgender mind but often also in our own. Good, bad, different, inferior, transitioned, too feminine, not masculine enough, *trying too hard* (or *not hard enough*), passing (or not passing), insubordinate, overturning gender or recapitulating it, whatever—the trans body is always required *to be something*, and is seen to be *doing something*. It must always bear this incredibly weight of social meaning—inevitably something strange. It can never just *be*, and among the things it can never be is simply normal.

In a way I still didn't understand. I had learned to experience my gender not as a private property of my body and identity, but as a kind of public possession that was being jointly managed in agreement with how the cisgender public thought about me.

In constantly trying to intuit how others were seeing me, I found my phenomenological sense of myself and my body often became unmoored, rotating through several different senses of how I looked and felt in quick succession, as I tried to match how I thought others were seeing me.

The term I use to describe this to myself is "strobing," but what it actually feels is like falling through a series of floors one after another. This is especially common when I'm being looked at in a group of cisgender strangers and I can't figure out how they're reading my body. My mind will cycle through a number of different settings on the Cisgender Inspection Dial, which is highly disorienting.

Sometimes I end up switching setting from one person to another, as some jock extends his hand to pump mine man-to-man, and then a friend walks up to ask, "And how are you ladies doing?" (I know, it sounds condescending even to me.)

It's a weird part of sex that this also affected my moments of intimacy with lovers. I was never sure how the person I was with saw me, and if they wanted the femme me, or the butch boy energy me? While clearly they saw me as an erotic partner, was it as another woman, a sort of woman who used to be male, an exotic transsexual? And the last thing I was going to do was interrupt our encounter mid-moan so they could fill out a survey.

I'm reminded here of Du Bois's concept in racism of "double consciousness," in which abjected subjects must stand apart from themselves to see how the dominant culture is perceiving them to survive. And also Sartre's *alienated man*, who "is vividly and constantly conscious of his body, not as it is for him, but as it is for the Other"—which he called the *body-for-others*.[86,87] Well, since childhood I had always had a body-for-others.

Undoing this required a double-act: detaching from how others saw me and, then, detaching from how I had learned *from* them to see myself. But how to know which one is *me*? And then I remind myself: it's the one that feels like *mine*, the one that feels "right," and that all the "other bodies" leave me feeling alienated and miserable.

In the end, I think that's all we have. It certainly should be all we need.

I look back now on when I was younger, struggling with transition, and looking forward to surgery; when everything seemed to be progressing, I had such naïve hopes, and time was a linear march forward. I'm constantly surprised today, all these years later, about how time seems to be circular, always doubling back on itself. As author Thomas Page McBee wrote, "Trans time isn't linear . . . many of us live in loops that double back on themselves. A second birth, a second death, two puberties, a collapsing of space-time that becomes, eventually, a kind of integration."[88]

The fact that I'm finally starting to close this particular circle in my seventies seems absurd. At this age, I'd imagined that one's growth and changing would be largely over, and all those gender demons with which I wrestled would have long ago retired from the ring. At this age, it fills me with awe at time's passage and the strange detours and eddies it makes. Struggling with gender is among the longest single arcs of continuous awareness in my life. I can still see myself sometimes—that cheerless, confused girl again of five or six—and I feel a strange, tender sadness rising gently inside me like smoke for this lonely child who never was, who lost so very much so very early and had no way of knowing that one day, decades and decades later, it would finally get better.

Surviving Sex

At one time, I was in love with a butch-y lover who remained indifferent to her breasts. She paid no attention to them when dressing or bathing, and, during our intimacy, she had no interest in them either. If I fondled them or kissed or sucked her nipples, she would smile tolerantly but nothing more. Eventually I stopped, because it aroused me, but not her, and so it began to feel vaguely like molesting her. When I asked her about this, she replied that she didn't mind it all and actually found it quite pleasant. She just didn't relate to having breasts and so didn't find having them caressed or sucked particularly erotic.

As I said, this pretty much described how I have tended to interact with my entire body during sex, while I mainly eroticized what was happening to my partner.

The change after surgery was stark. Coming with a penis felt like an orgasm that was occurring six inches in front of my body: nice, but distant, and not anything I was particularly connected to.

But having an orgasm with a clitoris and vagina with penetration was more like someone filling my entire pelvis with a hot liquid, and could often become so intense that it was difficult to breathe. Plemons notes that many surgeons believe that post-op trans women "will continue to have 'male orgasms.'"[89] They should try one. I doubt the existence of binary male/female orgasms, but whatever I have is obviously very different from before.

But if sex with a penis had always felt distant and detached, it also felt comfortably invulnerable. But having someone suddenly inside my body causing all this intense pleasures felt too intimate, too vulnerable, too intense. This all felt terribly unsafe: mentally, my trauma reaction would quickly kick in, and I'd space out and dissociate. Physically, I would try to control the sex as when I had a penis and was "driving," tightening obscure muscles that still lived in my groin in an effort to try to dictate the depth and pace of the interaction to control the sensations.

This deadened everything enough and gave me back a sense of control, but it didn't make for good sex. It has been a slow and different process finally allowing someone else to "drive," and allowing sensations their acts are producing in my body to come to me directly and unencumbered. All of this makes the sex much more intense, and the climaxes longer, and a marked sense of fulfillment afterward. But it is still occasionally terrifying. Because of this, I find I'm often much better at it and more relaxed for the feelings when by myself self-recreating.[90]

The fact that my new orgasms were sometimes so overwhelming raises some interesting questions, chief among them—*how*?

There's is no particular reason the pleasures of an *innie* should be so different than those of an *outie*. But, for me, the quality of erotic sensation with a vagina was totally different and infinitely better. This made little sense, since considering the donor site for the tissue butt, penetration shouldn't have been particularly pleasurable. In addition, my outer genital area now had considerably less surface area and nerve endings for available than before.

Perhaps, part of the pleasure was just that I was able to finally eroticize the acts in which my body was participating. As Prosser has argued about trans men, perhaps this works as well as it does because some trans women have a kind of "psychic vagina" (whatever that might be). It certainly wouldn't surprise my eight- or nine-year-old self in front of my parent's mirror.

Maybe it was also a sign of at last being able to make peace with my *junk*—although the word "simply" is doing a lot of heavy lifting here. Bettcher notes in "Trans Women and 'Interpretive Intimacy'" that for trans people, sex often requires sensitive negotiation with potential partners over what one's body means, how one wants it to be read, how one wants it eroticized.[91] I find for sex—whether with others or when pleasuring myself—I've had to repeatedly conduct many of these same negotiations with myself and the Committee.

In any case, I assume lots of postoperative women go through a process of reintegrating their new genital configurations into their bodily schema and thence into the vast intimacy of sex. And yet critical theory tells us almost nothing about process, or about how post-op arousal, orgasm, and eroticism function are even possible.

As Malatino notes in "Future Fatigue" about transition and "Hormone Time," this horizon of the long-sought "harmony between the felt and the perceived body" always "seems to be infinitely receding," always just over the next hill.[92] So that one is never entirely post-transition, but merely postoperative.

Trans bodies are always in a state of becoming; as Howitt puts it: sex may initially be felt as a struggle to resist the ways social contexts territorialize and specify what "normal" bodies do, a kind of *dysphoric wounding* that cycles through rounds of trial and error, with dissembling being followed by new assemblages, until at last we arrive at a more pleasureful sexuality and erotic embodiment. But for many of us, even this successful reintegration is not linear, not a destination, but a journey of ascending circular spirals that (like mine) can last a lifetime.[93]

Sensation and Accomplishment

When I had surgery, I expected my new vagina to feel—I don't know—vaginal. It didn't. I realized this the moment I came to groggy half-awakeness and was instantly, massively disappointed. As I said earlier, while I don't know what a factory-installed vagina feels, I do know what a penis feels like. The doctors had promised to save as many nerve endings as possible and had obviously done their job: the sensation was exactly like someone had removed all the bone and muscle from my arm so they could stitch all the left-over nerve endings to my shoulder.

I still felt all the same things, but just in a strangely and unpleasantly cramped way. Weirdly, I could visualize the places on what used to be my lady-dick, and figure out where those nerves now lived in my new genitals. But it was highly unsettling and dysphoric; as the novelty quicky wore off, I stopped doing it.

Over time, this sense has pretty much left me, and now everything feels quite vaginal.[94] But it does make me wonder if cis women and men are feeling pretty much the same things, just differently arranged. After all, all human genitals originate in the same neonatal tissue.

A strange by-product of postsurgical embodiment is that for several decades, whenever I'm deeply asleep and need to urinate (which, as I get older, is regrettably often), my brain seems to need to create a reason why I'm not answering the call. So often it would situate me in a Women's Room, where I wasn't peeing because I still had a penis, and—making matters worse—the other women were all circling me and very angry. This was extremely distressing to wake up to over and over and has thankfully mostly stopped.

But I was reminded of this when reading "One Man's Junk" in Trystan Cotton's book *Hung Jury*, in which Declan writes, "I'd have nightmares about strangers angrily grabbing my crotch and shouting at me that I had no penis."[95] It makes me wonder if the specter of overflowing cishostility is a common traumatic nightmare among transitioning trans people. If so, it is a sad fact.

If my own experience is any guide, the process of reintegrating new genital configurations is fraught and challenging enough and is hampered by the specters of fear and internalized self-hate and cisgender skepticism and hostility.

It's still so challenging for me, that I increasingly see trans embodiment during sex as a kind of gendered accomplishment. Pre-op, post-op, non-op, we "retool," rename, and invent new signifying economies; explore novel sexual practices (*muffing*, anyone?); assimilate erotic toys and devices and/or don specific apparel; negotiate terms and technique with prospective lovers; integrate entirely new physical sensations and transform our sense of existing ones—all to better create satisfying pleasures and embody our sexual selves. And we do all this in the face of massive disconfirmatory pressure from family, media, medicine, TERFs, and even skeptical partners (as those of us who've had potential partners literally get up and walk out know all too well).

As Howitt asks, "How does a sex act or body part that once caused great discomfort transform into a pleasureful or ecstatic experience? How can a lifelong dissatisfaction with a particular bodily appendage transform into the deep and profound acceptance of the parts that were there all along? Why does the surgical alteration of bodies rapidly expand pleasure capacities?"[96] And, I would add, how is all this not miraculous and worthy of the profound scholarly attention?

It was easy for me to become aroused looking at someone. But to actually *have* sex with them and stay present for it, to give myself over to the sensations they were producing, to be fulfilled by sex with a body whose erotic sensations had been radically reconfigured and with genitalia I was still learning my way around, and to have all this integrated into my bodily schema and have all this come together flawlessly at the moment of greatest intimacy with and exposure to another human being is a kind of crazy achievement. It may even be a kind of resistance, one that refutes the epistemic violence of the cisgender gaze, its aesthetic hegemony, and what Malatino calls its "repeated, persistent, and dogged misrecognition" and replaces it— even if only temporarily—with the releasing anonymity of pleasure and orgasm.[97]

Prosser may be right about this working at all because I already had a vagina-type body in my head. But even if that's so, being reembodied with one still took a lot of work, a lot of trial and error, and a long journey with many dead-end, plateaus, and setbacks leavened by irregular bouts of progress—and then those luminous moments when I am temporarily, unexpectedly, giddily present during sex and everything aligns, and sex is good for a change. If it's still not exactly an everyday occurrence, but it *is* nice knowing it's always out there, somewhere, waiting for me to rediscover it. And maybe one day, it will come to stay.

A Field in Exile?

Whatever the ontology of the transsexed body, I think it is highly unlikely that epistemologic tools we have—not essentialism, not social constructionism, not the *wrong-body* or the *coat-rack* model— are up to the task of unpacking it. I'm not an academic, much less a philosopher, but when I try to think through questions like these about trans sensation, embodiment, and pleasure, I can almost feel the wheels on the old postmodern/queer theory/trans study models creaking and about to come off.

I don't believe we know anything about trans people. The epistemologies we have were not designed for them and can only be applied to them with great difficulty. This is why we end up with made-up categories and words like "Transgender" and "Transsexual," and explanations like being trapped in the wrong body, having some immutable biological gender identity, or the desire to "transition" "from one sex to the other"—things I suspect almost *none* of us said to ourselves as children when we discovered there was something different about us or think to ourselves today as adults—particularly when we're in the midst of sex.

Such things are artifacts of cislogocentrism, and thus they are dandy for explaining ourselves and making our lives legible within the demand characteristics imposed by cisgender politics. But I doubt they tell very much that is intrinsic about us. And to express something more truly trans-centric, we will likely need a trans-centric epistemology that originates closer to home.

I am the first to admit that I have no idea what this might be and that it's a job for smarter heads than mine. But after writing about trans and queer theory for thirty years, I imagine I can tell that it feels like when an epistemology has run its course and come to the of its road, when it no longer has anything new to offer in answer to the questions to which it has been applied.

Some trans academics considered Chu's naughty girl op-ed in the *Times* about sex and her vagina-to-be so striking that they opined it might herald a "second wave" in trans discourse.[98] Yet all it really did was to say what we already know but don't speak: that bottom surgery, while important and desirable for many, does not instantly transform our lives into puppy dogs and moonbeams.

This does not qualify as a shattering insight for transsexuals, and thus all Chu did was "say the quiet part out loud"—disabusing a cis audience of a fairy tale they have for too long found comforting to believe and to hear us recite for them.

But cisgender people don't really think of us as women anyway, so they enjoy thinking that surgically "changing sexes" to be "like them" will make us happy. Because who wouldn't want to be cisgender, or at least cisgender-Lite, if they had the chance? And wanting to be anything other than cisgender also might force them to question how they essentialize the binary qualities of their own bodies.

So no, Virginia—there is no Surgical Santa Claus. Transsexual women don't get vaginas to make them happy—transsexual women get vaginas because they are women.

This is yet another area of intentional cisgender ignorance, a kind of intentional obtuseness about trans, along with detransitioning, the need for medical gatekeeping, and so on. Writing of racism, scholar Charles Mills termed a deliberate non-knowing by a dominant culture as an *epistemology of ignorance*. It is similar to what Bettcher termed a "willful blindness, a patent disregard."[99,100]

Mills was not referring to simply not knowing a fact—*object ignorance*, or being misinformed about it—*factual ignorance*. Rather, he meant a calculated and deliberate not-knowing to avoid recognizing obvious truths that are inconvenient and threaten prevailing hierarchies.[101]

In many ways, Mill's insight might also be applied to gender, to the many intentional ignorances cisgender society indulges in so as not to have to grapple with realities of us and our bodies: there is not one ignorance, but many.

Among them, there is actually nothing the slightest bit special about transsexuals. Yes, we change body parts, but so do people with burns, cancer, war wounds, and congenital conditions—and also heart, kidney, and lung transplants. Our primary and secondary sex characteristics change markedly changes, but so do those of every adolescent. And while there is, unfortunately, a *lot* about us that is special politically, there is nothing at all about us that is ontologically special. Being transsexed is actually pretty pedestrian, even boring. It's just cisgender politics that keeps us from being recognized as such.

Another novel thing about Chu's piece was that it spoke publicly about transgender genitals. Again, the fact that we have genitalia also does not qualify as a shattering insight among transsexual women. What *was* new was reading one of us write openly about them and breaking our self-imposed silence.

As Foucault famously noted, in any hegemonic discourse, there is not one but many silences. And among trans academia, this includes not writing about our genitals, our sexuality, our phenomenology and erotic embodiment, and the complexities of intimate encounters. We don't speak much of this to one another much, and we certainly don't speak or write much about it to the cisgender public (especially at a time when many of us are fleeing to *sanctuary states*). It is of a piece with trans studies' current anti-transsexual moment, when everything must be mobile and multiple and contingent and nothing so gauche and tangible as our groins, their erotic activities, and the frequent complications.

As Bettcher notes, trans studies remains a field which

> must be undertaken with some caution: There's a danger in even *going there* (or at least going there publicly) since what we can also be weaponized against us. Indeed, one of the functions of this threat is precisely this kind foreclosure of self-understanding, of illumination . . . keeping us off balance [and] threatening to use our own self-critique against us, rendering philosophical reflection nearly impossible.[102]

She concludes from this that it only points how vital it is to persevere and contest this.

In seeking feedback for my thoughts about doing a book like this on trans sexuality and embodiment, I spoke with three well-known academics in trans studies whose work I deeply respect. I was astonished to find that the four of us, who have all published widely, had had many similar experiences around sex and even shared many of the same questions. Yet all of us had remained publicly silent about this. Moreover, all three offered me some formulation of the following warning: "You know, it will be used against us."

These kinds of self-imposed silences are examples of what philosopher Kristie Dotson, speaking of Black feminism, has called *testimonial smothering*—which occurs when subjects avoid speaking their truths because of fear of punishment by the dominant culture.[103]

When it comes to sexuality and erotic embodiment, our shared silence about things all of us know means that each of us is forced to wrestle with such issues in private.

The threat of retribution hangs over transgender academics, discouraging them from interrogating our own lusts, pleasures, sexuality, kinks, and erotic embodiment. As David Bell puts it, university departments make it "easier to write about sexual identities and politics than sexual practices, easier to get published on gay gentrification than on fisting"—and of course easier to write about trans people having gender identities than having sex, the *do-ing* of gender rather than the *do-ing* of pleasure.[104] And for untenured scholars, this is amplified by the additional threats of economic loss, and professional respect and viability.

Thus, many trans academics labor under great self-restraint when they do venture to write about such topics, about which they have very strong feelings and which they must labor to keep out of their work. They rightfully fear that allowing their feelings into their writing risks academic retribution, and puncturing the appearance of professional objectivity that leads to peer-reviewed journals failing to take it seriously. I have had friends who said they had extremely intense emotional experiences when writing papers about genitals, sexuality, or erotic embodiment, but kept it all out of their submitted work lest it be dismissed as confessional, biased, overly subjective, and unprofessional.

Dotson also coined the term *testimonial quieting* to refer to the ways that abjected people suppress speaking their truths because they fear it will be disconfirmed and discarded by the dominant culture. While trans studies is very good at deconstructing the ways that culture imposes silences upon us, we have been less effective at interrogate the many ways we now impose such silences on ourselves.[105]

One highly respected New York academic was explaining to me their need to maintain their academic *omerta* on sexuality, even as their own transgender partner was about to undergo bottom surgery shortly, and both were desperate for information about what to expect in terms of her postoperatively genital embodiment and particularly her sexual functioning and response.

Even though my surgery was about 100 years ago, I spent an hour with them sharing details of my own experience, wondering how it was that none of us could refer to single trans studies paper or book which directly addressed their questions. Moreover, since they both knew plenty of transsexual women, it meant they also didn't feel comfortable posing these kinds of uber-intimate questions to any of them. And predictably, the woman hadn't even discussed her sexual expectations, fears, and priorities with the surgeon who was about to operate on her body—who had also predictably not asked her about these.

How is it that, as we close in on nearly a century since the first widely known "sex change surgery," any transfeminine academic worth their salt can deconstruct *the signifying practices of phallogocentric economy with its inevitable tropes and metaphors of heteronormativity*, but this woman was still so desperate for any information on how her body and sexuality would function postoperatively that she and her partner were reduced to picking my brains over a phone call only months before she went under the knife?

As Howitt has noted:

> The dearth of sex research has left trans people (and perhaps vitally, their care providers) with very little knowledge about the visceral, fleshy, fluid functions of the "messy materiality" of the (trans) sexed body (Binnie, 1997), and how it fucks. As demonstrated in

research into disabled sexualities (Santos and Santos, 2018), when it comes to bodies that defy normative expectations, "the lack of specialized information about sexuality . . . leads to ignorance and fear."[106]

It is hard to think of another area so intrinsic to transgender experience in which we indulge in so much testimonial smothering. It makes one wonder what other unspoken subject areas are out there about transsexuals, crossdressers, the intersex/DSD, or nonbinary folks; whatever they are, I'm betting they will be transformative.

Our silences and the fear that causes them *feel* personal, because each of us experiences it alone. But these persistent silences and avoidances, this reluctance to investigate some of our most obvious and pressing and universal needs—even in the face of acute personal and professional awareness of them—are completely political.

All such silences are political, just as the trans silence about them is political. They concern particular classes of things which cannot be said publicly, even when we have the credibility to say them and can make socially legible truth statements about them. They result from specific structures of power, serve specific agendas, and are the result of specific kinds of structures of fear that have been erected to preserve specific hierarchies.

They are a characteristic of us as a community, and they are signs of a shared and continuing but unspoken communal trauma. They result from the deliberate discouraging of the pursuit and annunciation of specific kinds of trans knowledge and the speaking of specific trans discourses.

And this makes it more difficult for us to fully recognize ourselves and to fully recognize one another—the kind of *hermeneutical liberation* of which George and Goguen wrote so passionately.

Because of this smothering, as with my academic friends in New York, seventy years after America's first "sex change surgery," each of us is *still* forced to work out such things (or fail to) alone, in ignorance and isolation, learning about critical issues in sexuality and erotic embodiment from friends or surfing online, reinventing this wheel of knowledge over and over again because as a field we cannot speak of them to ourselves.

For all our just political anger and obvious theoretical prowess, we remain, to put it perhaps too bluntly, still largely *cowed* before the specter of cisgender animus in these areas.

As the invaluable Bettcher notes, it is hard to think new thoughts when the fear or the reality of constant attacks keep you in a defensive posture.[107] Or, as philosopher Marilyn Frye explains, "We can't imagine what we can't face, and we can't face what we can't imagine. . . . [W]e have to dare to rely on ourselves to make meaning and we have to imagine ourselves beings capable of that: capable of weaving the web of meaning which will hold us in some kind of intelligibility."[108]

Trans studies lacks this intelligibility about the transgender body and its intimate functions. In many ways, it is not even searching for it yet.

So we remain strangers to this part of our selves, only our bodies darkly through a cisgender lens that distorts that which is seen.

Perhaps that is why voices like Binnie's or Chu's resonate with so many in the community. Because we hope that in the end we will at last make that long, elusive peace with being able to speak and think and theorize our junk.

As Cherríe Moraga declared in the essay with which this book opened, what we keep hidden eventually becomes painful and deformed. And thus, in important ways trans studies remains a field-in-exile, a field-in-waiting—covering its eyes from its own insights, unwilling and still waiting to speak openly and fully about the lives it theorizes, the bodies it inhabits, and the acts they undertake.

NOTES

Foreword

1 Andrea Long Chu, "The Pink," *N+1*, Spring 2019, https://www.nplusonemag
.com/issue-34/politics/the-pink/.

2 Gabriel Mac, "My Penis, Myself I Didn't Need a Penis to be a Man. But I
Needed One to be Me," *Intelligencer*, December 20, 2021, https://nymag.com/
intelligencer/article/gabriel-mac-essay.html.

3 Florence Ashley, "Genderfucking as a Critical Legal Methodology," *McGill
Law Journal*, December 6, 2023, Forthcoming. Available at SSRN https://ssrn
.com/abstract=4656170.

4 Cohen Cathy, "Punks. Bulldaggers and Welfare Queens: The Radical
Potential of Queer Policies?" *GLQ: A Journal of Lesbian and Gay Studies* 3,
no. 4 (1997): 437–-465.

5 Blas Radi, "On Trans* Epistemology," *Transgender Studies Quarterly* 6, no. 1
(February 1, 2019): 43–63, https://doi.org/10.1215/23289252-7253482.

6 Annys Shin, "6 Key Takeaways From the Post-KFF Survey of Transgender
Americans," *Washington Post*, April 13, 2023, https://www.washingtonpost
.com/dc-md-va/2023/03/23/takeaways-post-kff-survey/.

7 Anna Brown, "About 5% of Young Adults in the U.S. Say Their Gender Is
Different From Their Sex Assigned at Birth," *Pew Research Center*, June
7, 2022, https://www.pewresearch.org/short-reads/2022/06/07/about-5
-of-young-adults-in-the-u-s-say-their-gender-is-different-from-their-sex
-assigned-at-birth/.

Chapter 1

1 Cassius Adair and Aren Aizura, "'The Transgender Craze Seducing Our
[Sons]'; or, All the Trans Guys Are Just Dating Each Other," *Transgender*

Studies Quarterly 9, no. 1 (February 1, 2022): 44–64, https://doi.org/10
.1215/23289252-9475509.

2 Florence Ashley, *Gender/Fucking: The Pleasures and Politics of Living in a Gendered Body* (Google Books, n.d.), Clash Books, 2023. https://books
.google.com/books/about/Gender_Fucking_the_Pleasures_and_Politic
.html?id=egqSzwEACAAJ.

3 Billy Huff, "Thinking Trans/Sex: Erotic Justice and the Trans-Subject," *QED: A Journal in GLBTQ Worldmaking* 10, no. 1 (Spring 2023): 123–43.

4 Amber Hollibaugh and Cherríe Moraga, "What We're Rollin Around in Bed With: Sexual Silences in Feminism," in *Feminism and Pornography*, ed. Drucilla Cornell (Oxford University Press eBooks, 2000), 587–99, https://
doi.org/10.1093/oso/9780198782506.003.0034.

5 C. Jacob Hale, "Leatherdyke Boys and Their Daddies: How to Have Sex Without Women or Men," *Social Text*, no. 52/53 (1997): 223–36, https://doi
.org/10.2307/466741https://www.jstor.org/stable/466741.

6 Morty Diamond, *Trans/Love: Radical Sex, Love & Relationships Beyond the Gender Binary* (Manic D Press, San Francisco, U.S. 2011).

7 S. Stryker, "Dungeon Intimacies: The Poetics of Transsexual Sadomasochism," *Parallax* 14, no. 1 (2008): 36–47, https://doi.org/10.1080
/13534640701781362.

8 "Lou Sullivan Collection—Digital Transgender Archive," n.d., https://www
.digitaltransgenderarchive.net/col/j6731380t.

9 "In Defense of the Tranny Chaser," in 2020; Billy Huff, "On [Be] Coming in Boystown," *Journal of Autoethnography* 3, no. 4 (October 1, 2022): 427–44; and Huff, Billy. "Thinking Trans/Sex: Erotic Justice and the Trans-Subject." *QED: A Journal in GLBTQ Worldmaking* 10, no. 1 (2023): 123–143.

10 In addition, Lucie Fielding's, *Trans Sex: Clinical Approaches to Trans Sexualities and Erotic Embodiment*, while aimed at clinicians, also offers many practical tips for trans people working through their own sexuality issues. Lucie Fielding, *Trans Sex: Clinical Approaches to Trans Sexualities and Erotic Embodiments* (Milton Park, Abingdon UK: Routledge, 2021).

11 Ashley, *Gender/Fucking*.

12 "Nerve Endings: The New Trans Erotic: 9780990452874: Hill-Meyer (Editor), Tobi: Books," n.d., https://www.amazon.com/Nerve-Endings-New
-Trans-Erotic/dp/0990452875.

13 Kayla Kumari Upadhyaya, "Autostraddle," *Autostraddle*, n.d., https://www .autostraddle.com/.

14 Trystan Cotten, *Below the Below: Genital Talk by Men of Trans Experience* (Oakland: Transgress Press, 2016).

15 Trystan T. Cotten, *Hung Jury: Testimonies of Genital Surgery by Transsexual Men* (Oakland: Transgress Press, 2012).

16 Elijah Adiv Edelman and Lal Zimman, "Boycunts and Bonus Holes: Trans Men's Bodies, Neoliberalism, and the Sexual Productivity of Genitals," *Journal of Homosexuality* 61, no. 5 (2014): 673–90, https://doi.org/10.1080 /00918369.2014.870438.

17 My experiences are obviously and sadly markedly different from those of Florence Ashley, who reports in her book "Gender/Fucking" on the number of nudes she's traded with other trans academics and dates she has secured with them through direct messaging.

18 Personal communication with author, 2022.

19 Emily Grabham, "Citizen Bodies, Intersex Citizenship," *Sexualities* 10, no. 1 (February 1, 2007): 29–48, https://doi.org/10.1177/1363460707072951.

20 Natalie Reed, "The Eunuch, The Rapist, The Whore And The Child Who Simply Knew," *Freethought Blogs*, October 11, 2012, https:// freethoughtblogs.com/nataliereed/2012/10/11/the-eunuch-the-rapist-the -whore-and-the-child-who-simply-knew/.

21 Ashley, *Gender/Fucking*.

22 Susan Styker, "Dungeon Intimacies," in *When Monsters Speak* (Duke University Press eBooks, 2024), 58–71, https://doi.org/10.1215 /9781478059462-007.

23 Julia Serano, "Penises, Privilege, and Feminist & LGBTQ+ Purity Politics," *Medium*, July 18, 2023, https://juliaserano.medium.com/penises-privilege -and-feminist-lgbtq-purity-politics-bafd1f25fe3e.

24 Eric Plemons and Chris Straayer, "Introduction," *Transgender Studies Quarterly* 5, no. 2 (May 1, 2018): 164–73, https://doi.org/10.1215/23289252 -4348605.

25 Jack Halberstam, José Esteban Muñoz, and David L. Eng, "What's Queer about Queer Studies Now?" *Social Text* 23, nos. 3–4 (2005): 84–5.

26 For instance, see: Filippo Maria Nimbi, Giacomo Ciocca, Erika Limoncin, Lilybeth Fontanesi, Ünal Batuhan Uysal, Matthew Flinchum, Renata

Tambelli, Emmanuele Angelo Jannini, and Chiara Simonelli, "Sexual Desire and Fantasies in the LGBT+ Community: Focus on Lesbian Women and Gay Men," *Current Sexual Health Reports* 12, no. 3 (2020): 153–61, https://doi.org/10.1007/s11930-020-00263-7.

27 This reticence is not unique to queers but of course occurs across large areas of academia and even the public. Americans are especially bad in this area. While we're inundated in sex in media, there's still a paucity of actual basic education on sex, and not just among school children. Most of us adults still don't even know the right words for our sex organs. Studies show that only about a third of women can correctly identify the clitoris on a body diagram—and just half of women aged twenty-six to thirty-five are able to label the vagina accurately, Perhaps this is not surprising, since most sex education and discussion of genitals in the United States is around reproduction—which mainly involves penises and uteruses—with almost no attention paid to actual pleasure. {CITE Morgan, Viva la Vulva.}

28 Dinitia Smith, "'Queer Theory' Is Entering the Literary Mainstream," *The New York Times*, January 17, 1998, https://www.nytimes.com/1998/01/17/books/queer-theory-is-entering-the-literary-mainstream.html.

29 Susan Stryker, "Transgender Studies: Queer Theory's Evil Twin," *GLQ: A Journal of Lesbian and Gay Studies* 10, no. 2 (2004): 212–15, muse.jhu.edu/article/54599.

30 Filippo Maria Nimbi, Giacomo Ciocca, Erika Limoncin, Lilybeth Fontanesi, Ünal Batuhan Uysal, Matthew Flinchum, Renata Tambelli, Emmanuele Angelo Jannini, and Chiara Simonelli, "Sexual Desire and Fantasies in the LGBT+ Community: A Focus on Bisexuals, Transgender, and Other Shades of the Rainbow," *Current Sexual Health Reports* 12, no. 3 (2020): 162–9, https://doi.org/10.1007/s11930-020-00262-8.

31 Stryker, "Transgender Studies."

32 Stryker, "Transgender Studies."

33 *TSQ: Transgender Studies Quarterly* 1, no. 1–2 (May 2014).Duke University Press.

34 T. Cooper, *Real Man Adventures* (McSweeney's, 2012).

35 Mira Bellwether, *Fucking Trans Women*, no. 0 (Iowa: Self-published, 2010).

36 Huff, "Thinking Trans/Sex," 123–43 (Article).

37 ResearchGate, "Transgender Studies, or How to Do Things with Trans*," June 1, 2020, https://www.researchgate.net/publication/341938157 _Transgender_Studies_or_How_to_Do_Things_with_Trans.

38 Huff, "On [Be]coming in Boystown."

39 Andrea Long Chu and Emmett Harsin Drager, "After Trans Studies," *Transgender Studies Quarterly* 6, no. 1 (February 1, 2019): 103–16, https://doi.org/10.1215/23289252-7253524.

40 Gayle S. Rubin, "Thinking Sex: Notes for a Radical Theory of the Politics of Sexuality," in *Culture, Society and Sexuality* (Routledge eBooks, 2007), 166–203, https://doi.org/10.4324/9780203966105-21.

41 "Stone Butch Blues: Leslie Feinberg: Amazon.com: Books," 1993.

42 Andrea Long Chu and Anastasia Berg, "Wanting Bad Things," *The Point Magazine*, July 18, 2018 , https://thepointmag.com/dialogue/wanting-bad -things-andrea-long-chu-responds-amia-srinivasan/.

43 Leslie Feinberg, *Stone Butch Blues: A Novel*, 1993, https://blindhypnosis .com/stone-butch-blues-pdf-leslie-feinberg.html.

44 R. E. Wallace, "As a Non-Binary Person I Struggle to Feel Desirable in Today's Society," *HuffPost UK* (blog), June 12, 2018, https://www .huffingtonpost.co.uk/entry/non-binary-desirability_uk_5c07fffee4b0bf8 13ef36910?utm_source=pocket_saves.

45 I'm obviously using highly dimorphic examples for clarity and simplicity. This is not to imply that we should understand bodies or their sexuality this way, nor that it is the only way to understand these.

46 Talia Mae Bettcher, "When Selves Have Sex: What the Phenomenology of Trans Sexuality Can Teach About Sexual Orientation," *Journal of Homosexuality* 61, no. 5 (April 9, 2014): 605–20, https://doi.org/10.1080 /00918369.2014.865472.

47 Butler, Judith. 2006. *Gender Trouble: Feminism and the Subversion of Identity*. Routledge Classics, 9780415389556: Butler, Judith: Books.

48 Perhaps surprisingly, Butler has been quite public and open about how their own early identification as a lesbian, the emergence of sex radicalism among 1980s feminism, and the ensuring Sex Wars were determinative in her thinking. Her ArtForum interview titled "The Body You Want" is a good example of this.

49 "Gender Trouble: Feminism and the Subversion of Identity (Routledge Classics): 9780415389556: Butler, Judith: Books."

50 Certainly there are many pop books—John Rechy's *Numbers* and *City of Night* come to mind here—about gay sex outlaw culture, but I'm talking more about the ways we mobilized our sexuality in intimate encounters.

51 Eric D. Plemons, "It Is as It Does: Genital Form and Function in Sex Reassignment Surgery," *The Journal of Medical Humanities* 35, no. 1 (December 11, 2013): 37–55, https://doi.org/10.1007/s10912-013-9267-z.

52 Andrea Long Chu, "Opinion | My New Vagina Won't Make Me Happy," *New York Times*, November 24, 2018, https://www.nytimes.com/2018/11/24/opinion/sunday/vaginoplasty-transgender-medicine.html.

53 Personal communication with author, 2001.

54 Huff, "Thinking Trans/Sex," 123–43.

55 Just to be clear, I am not arguing that this is an essential property if any act or organ is independent of how we construct them.

57 George Chauncey, *Gay New York: Gender, Urban Culture, and the Making of the Gay Male World, 1890–1940* (New York: Basic Books, 1994).

58 "Paisley Currah: 'On Judith Butler and Jules Gill-Peterson,'" *The Yale Review*, March 3, 2024, https://yalereview.org/article/paisley-currah-judith-butler-jules-gill-peterson.

59 Lisa Duggan, *The Twilight of Equality?: Neoliberalism, Cultural Politics, and the Attack on Democracy* (Boston: Beacon Press, 2003).

60 There is a *transnormativity* of course, but it's a very different dynamic and refers to the pressure to fulfill normative socio-medical expectations for how to be "properly" transgender. These generally include transsexual-related experiences such as feelings of being "trapped in the wrong body," getting diagnosed with gender dysphoria, taking hormones and having surgery, and presenting with a dimorphic cisnormative gender expression. See: Austin H. Johnson, "Transnormativity: A New Concept and Its Validation through Documentary Film About Transgender Men," *Sociological Inquiry* 86, no. 4 (July 6, 2016): 465–91, https://doi.org/10.1111/soin.12127.

61 Boundary. "Transgender Studies Today: An Interview with Susan Stryker," *Boundary 2*, August 20, 2014, https://www.boundary2.org/2014/08/transgender-studies-today-an-interview-with-susan-stryker/.

62 Boundary. "Transgender Studies Today."

63 Here are the searches I ran, for those inclined to confirm them for themselves.

allintitle: X source:journal source:of source:homosexuality
allintitle: X source:journal source:of source:lesbian source:studies
allintitle: X source:gay source:and source:lesbian source:studies
allintitle: X source:GLQ

64 Black poets like Essex Hemphill and Joseph Beam also wrote very specifically about gay male sexuality, at times in verse, although that would probably be considered more artistic than academic works.

65 Stryker, "Transgender Studies."

66 Halberstam, Muñoz, and Eng, "What's Queer about Queer Studies Now?"

67 Cáel M. Keegan, "Getting Disciplined: What's Trans* About Queer Studies Now?" *Journal of Homosexuality* 67, no. 3 (October 22, 2018): 384–97, https://doi.org/10.1080/00918369.2018.1530885.

68 Henry S. Rubin, "Phenomenology as Method in Trans Studies," *GLQ* 4, no. 2 (January 1, 1998): 263–81, https://doi.org/10.1215/10642684-4-2-263.

69 As one reviewer was kind enough to remind me, there is a robust subgroup of academics who study gay sexuality through online dating behavior via apps like Grinder and Tinder, and so on.

70 Of course, the pro-sex feminists of the Lesbian Sex Wars who theorized BD, SM, and butch/femme among other practices were initially marked exceptions.

71 Other than to argue that they should not be defined by them of course.

72 Eve Kosofsky Sedgwick, *Epistemology of the Closet* (Oakland CA: University of California Press, 1990).

73 David Valentine, "'We're Not about Gender': The Uses of 'Transgender,'" in *Out in Theory: The Emergence of Lesbian and Gay Anthropology,* ed. Lewin, E., & Leap, W. (Urbana: University of Illinois Press, 2002), 222–45.

74 Tellingly, over the years GLB was transposed to LGB, in order to foreground lesbians who had been too long submerged or excluded from gay rights, and might be considered more vulnerable to erasure. However, no such acronymic magic was applied when appending the T.

75 David Valentine, "'I Went to Bed With My Own Kind Once': The Erasure of Desire in the Name of Identity," *Language & Communication* 23, no. 2 (April 1, 2003): 123–38, https://doi.org/10.1016/s0271-5309(02)00045-9.

76 Valentine, "'We're Not about Gender': The Uses of 'Transgender.'"

77 Valentine, "'I Went to Bed With My Own Kind Once.'"

78 Valentine, "'We're Not about Gender': The Uses of 'Transgender.'"

79 Valentine, "'We're Not about Gender': The Uses of 'Transgender.'"

80 David Valentine, *Imagining Transgender: An Ethnography of a Category* (Durham NC: Duke University Press, 2007).

81 Some transitioned individuals in the United States also refuse the label "trans," because they feel it adds a qualifier to or otherwise dilutes their being women or men.

82 Anna Brown, "About 5% of Young Adults in the U.S. Say Their Gender Is Different From Their Sex Assigned at Birth." Pew Research Center, A June 7, 2022. https://www.pewresearch.org/short-reads/2022/06/07/about-5 -of-young-adults-in-the-u-s-say-their-gender-is-different-from-their-sex -assigned-at-birth/.

83 David Valentine, *Imagining Transgender: An Ethnography of a Category* (Durham NC: Duke University Press, 2020).

84 Valentine, "'We're Not about Gender': The Uses of 'Transgender.'"

85 Valentine, *Imagining Transgender*.

86 This is ironic, since their primary move has been doing so in order to deconstruct hetero- and cis-normativity.

87 Valentine, *Imagining Transgender*.

88 Valentine, *Imagining Transgender*.

89 To be fair, many of the techniques for GAS vaginoplasties were first developed and perfected on cisgender women who lost their vaginas through injury or disease, so in that sense one could say it still predates us, although presumably they had very different life experiences in their bodies getting to that point.

90 To be fair, most vaginoplasty techniques were first developed for and perfected on cisgender women whose vaginas were impaired due to injury or disease, so there was some, albeit very recent, precedent.

91 Laura Horak, "Trans on YouTube," *Transgender Studies Quarterly* 1, no. 4 (November 1, 2014): 572–85, https://doi.org/10.1215/23289252-2815255.

92 Declan, "One Man's Junk," in Trystan T. Cotten, *Hung Jury: Testimonies of Genital Surgery by Transsexual Men* (Oakland: Transgress Press, 2012).

93 Lal Zimman, "The Discursive Construction of Sex," in *Queer Excursions: Retheorizing Binaries in Language, Gender, and Sexuality* (Oxford University Press eBooks, 2014), 13–34, https://doi.org/10.1093/acprof:oso /9780199937295.003.0002.

94 Hari Ziyad, "3 Reasons Why Folks Who Don'T 'Look' Non-Binary Can Still Be Non-Binary," *Everyday Feminism*, May 18, 2016, https:// everydayfeminism.com/2016/05/still-non-binary/.

95 H. Howitt, "How We Fuck: Assembling Intimacy-as-Method to Research Trans Sex Practices," *Gender, Place & Culture* 31, no. 4 (2023): 523–42, https://doi.org/10.1080/0966369X.2023.2182738.

96 Ashley, "Genderfucking as a Critical Legal Methodology."

97 Personal communication with author, 2023.

98 Bellwether, *Fucking Trans Women*.

99 Bellwether explains that she uses the word "penis" for her own genitals, not to define them for every other trans woman, but simply for easy of communication.

100 https://www.autostraddle.com/muffing-101/.

101 This technique is certainly not entirely new in history and is known to experts in sexuality but it's safe to say it's still obscure enough to remain unknown to the general public.

102 Miranda Fricker and Katharine Jenkins, "Epistemic Injustice, Ignorance, and Trans Experiences," 2017, https://doi.org/10.4324/9781315758152-23.

103 L. Zimman, "Transgender Language Reform: Some Challenges and Strategies for Promoting Trans-affirming, Gender-Inclusive Language," *Journal of Language and Discrimination* 1, no. 1 (2017): 84–105, https://doi .org/10.1558/jld.33139.

104 Talia Mae Bettcher and Laurie Shrage, "Trans Identities and First-Person Authority," in *You've Changed: Sex Reassignment and Personal Identity*, vol. 1 (2009), 98–120.

105 @kels_koch, "Parents Asking Kids What they Learnt in Schoo . . . l &#x1F 923;😂🤣🤣😂🤦&#x1F3 FD; #reels #parents #kids," *Instagram*, December 9, 2023, https://www .instagram.com/p/C0oN8hYtD5Y/.

106 Bellwether, *Fucking Trans Women.*

107 Femke Olyslager and Lynn Conway, "On the Calculation of the Prevalence of Transsexualism," *ResearchGate*, January 2007, https://www.researchgate .net/publication/237519830_On_the_Calculation_of_the_Prevalence_of _Transsexualism.

108 Lynn Conway, "Estimating the Prevalence of Transsexualism," January 30, 2001, https://ai.eecs.umich.edu/people/conway/TS/TSprevalence.html.

109 George R. Brown, "Transvestic Disorder," Merck Manual Professional Edition, July 12, 2023, https://www.merckmanuals.com/professional/ psychiatric-disorders/paraphilias-and-paraphilic-disorders/transvestic -disorder.

110 Jody L. Herman, Andrew R. Flores, and Kathryn K. O'Neill, "How Many Adults and Youth Identify as Transgender in the United States?" *The Williams Institute at UCLA School of Law,* June 2022, https:// williamsinstitute.law.ucla.edu/publications/trans-adults-united-states/.

111 Richard F. Docter and Virginia Prince, "Transvestism: A Survey of 1032 Cross-dressers," *Archives of Sexual Behavior* 26, no. 6 (January 1, 1997): 589–605, https://doi.org/10.1023/a:1024572209266.

112 Crossdressing is not an exclusively male activity, and history shows that there have always been female crossdressers, but the practices appear to be overwhelmingly practiced by men, for reasons which are beyond the scope of this book, and thus these have remained my focus here.

113 Of course there is a difference between arousal linked to wearing certain garments, and getting aroused simply by handling garments themselves, which some minority of adults (mostly males)—including crossdressers— do. Interestingly, although the first is completely common, only one of these is considered a "kink" (i.e., fetish) by psychiatry. In addition, Theorist Ciara Cremin notes that the term "crossdressing" has been often deployed as a "neutral" activity that doesn't involve sexual pleasure, while "transvestism" is often more explicitly linked to fetishism, See: Anon, "Amazon.com: Future is Feminine, The: Capitalism and the Masculine Disorder: 9781350149779: Cremin, Ciara: Books," https://www.amazon .com/Future-Feminine-Capitalism-Masculine-Disorder/dp/1350149772.

114 Wikipedia contributors, "Sexual Swelling," Wikipedia, April 6, 2024, https://en.wikipedia.org/wiki/Sexual_swelling.

115 Ciara Cremin, "Feminine Praxis," *Counterfutures* 8 (March 18, 2020): 99–128, https://doi.org/10.26686/cf.v8i0.6453.

116 Ciara Cremin, "Trans Woman Does Not Exist? Trans Otherness and the Feminine Spectre," *Sublation Magazine*, April 4, 2023, https://www .sublationmag.com/post/trans-woman-does-not-exist.

117 https://www.usatoday.com/story/entertainment/celebrities/2024/09/16/ steve-o-jackass-breast-implant-prank/75248735007/.

118 Fielding, *Trans Sex*.

119 Deborah L. Tolman, *Dilemmas of Desire: Teenage Girls Talk about Sexuality* (Cambridge, MA: Harvard University Press, 2002), https://doi.org/10.2307 /j.ctvjz838w.

120 Brody, "Desirability," *Tran Sex Zine Vol II*, May 2018, 1.

121 Fielding, *Trans Sex*.

122 Aren Z. Aizura, Marquis Bey, Toby Beauchamp, Treva Ellison, Jules Bill-Peterson, and Eliza Steinbock, "Thinking with Trans Now," *Social Text* 38, no. 4 (2020): 128.

123 The three papers were: (**Alison note**: two of the papers were duplicates). Mats Holmberg, Stefan Arver, and Cecilia Dhejne, "Supporting Sexuality and Improving Sexual Function in Transgender Persons," *Nature Reviews. Urology* 16, no. 2 (October 30, 2018): 121–39, https://doi.org /10.1038/s41585-018-0108-8. Salvador Vidal-Ortiz, "Queering Sexuality and Doing Gender: Transgender Men's Identification with Gender and Sexuality," in *Gendered Sexualities* (*Advances in Gender Research, Vol. 6*), ed. P. Gagné and R. Tewksbury (Emerald Group Publishing Limited, Leeds, April 4, 2005), 181–233, https://doi.org/10.1016/S1529-2126(02)80008-X.

124 J. A. Puckett, K. Glozier, D. Kimball, and R. Giffel, "A Systematic Review of Sexuality Measurement in Transgender and Gender Diverse Populations," *Psychology of Sexual Orientation and Gender Diversity* 8, no. 3 (2021): 276–91, https://doi.org/10.1037/sgd0000523.

125 "Paisley Currah: 'On Judith Butler and Jules Gill-Peterson,'" 2024.

126 Viviane Namaste, *Sex Change, Social Change: Reflections on Identity, Institutions, and Imperialism* (Toronto: Women's Press, 2005), 3.

127 Chu and Drager, "After Trans Studies."

128 Lucie Fielding. "Trans Sex. Clinical Approaches to Trans Sexualities and Erotic Embodiments," *Zeitschrift Für Sexualforschung* 36, no. 1 (March 1, 2023): 53–5, https://doi.org/10.1055/a-1999-9669.

129 Andrea Long Chu and Anastasia Berg. "Wanting Bad Things," *The Point Magazine*, July 18, 2018, https://thepointmag.com/dialogue/wanting-bad -things-andrea-long-chu-responds-amia-srinivasan/.

130 Harry Benjamin, "THE TRANSSEXUAL PHENOMENON*," *Transactions of the New York Academy of Sciences* 29, no. 4 Series II (February 1, 1967): 428–30, https://doi.org/10.1111/j.2164-0947.1967.tb02273.x.

131 Reed, "The Eunuch, The Rapist, The Whore And The Child Who Simply Knew."

132 Chu, "My New Vagina Won't Make Me Happy."

133 Huff, "Thinking Trans/Sex," 123–43.

134 Thinking over my own body modification(s), this could imply a distinction between those that were strictly functional (breasts, genitals) and do things, and those that were aesthetic (nose, Adam's apple). Although looking back, the latter were more political and merely aesthetic—I wanted to minimize being harassed, not hired, and so on over what might be perceived as a "too-masculine" appearance. In this connection, my doctors questioned the fact that I wanted very minor breast augmentation to go with the hormonal changes that had already taken place, since this was unique in their experience with trans women. I told them I didn't want my breasts to interfere with my basketball stroke, which was true at the time. Although today that is no longer true (now it's my tennis stroke).

135 For one remarkable exception, see: "A Proposed Inventory to Assess Changes in Orgasm Function of Transgender Patients Following Gender Affirming Treatments: Pilot Study" https://pubmed.ncbi.nlm.nih.gov /35472753/ Citation: Zaliznyak, Michael, Marie Lauzon, Jenna Stelmar, Nance Yuan, Shannon M. Smith, and Maurice M. Garcia, "A Proposed Inventory to Assess Changes in Orgasm Function of Transgender Patients Following Gender Affirming Treatments: Pilot Study," *Sexual Medicine* 10, no. 3 (April 23, 2022): 1–5, https://doi.org/10.1016/j.esxm.2022.100510.

136 Riki Wilchins, *Read My Lips: Sexual Subversion and the End of Gender* (Ithaca: Firebrand Books, 1997).

137 Sandra Mesics, "When Building a Better Vulva, Timing Is Everything," *Transgender Studies Quarterly* 5, no. 2 (May 1, 2018): 245–50, https://doi .org/10.1215/23289252-4348672.

138 When I broke down in tears after sitting alone and being grilled by the full thirty-three-person team, my assigned psychiatric social worker told me approvingly that I "looked very feminine."

139 Plemons, "It Is as It Does: Genital Form and Function in Sex Reassignment Surgery."

140 R. Curtis, A. Levy, J. Martin, K. Wylie, T. Reed, and B. Reed, *A Guide to Lower Surgery for Trans Men* (Gender Identity Research and Education Society (GIRES), 2015).

141 F. Ashley and C. Ells, "In Favor of Covering Ethically Important Cosmetic Surgeries: Facial Feminization Surgery for Transgender People," *The American Journal of Bioethics* 18, no. 12 (2018): 23–5, https://doi.org/10 .1080/15265161.2018.1531162.

142 "Supporting Trans & Nonbinary Clients In Experiencing Gender Euphoria," Center of Excellence on LGBTQ+ Behavioral Health Equity, *lgbtequity.org*, April 2023, https://lgbtqequity.org/wp-content/uploads/2023 /04/Gender-Euphoria-Tip-Sheet.pdf.

143 Ashley, *Gender/Fucking*.

144 Gayle S. Rubin, "Thinking Sex: Notes for a Radical Theory of the Politics of Sexuality," in *Culture, Society and Sexuality* (Routledge, 2002), 143–78.

145 Judith Butler, *Bodies That Matter* (London: Routledge eBooks, 2011), https://doi.org/10.4324/9780203828274.

146 Janet Halley, *Split Decisions: How and Why to Take a Break from Feminism* (Princeton: Princeton University Press, 2008).

147 This is not, of course, intended to be an exhaustive list, just to represent some of the works for which these authors were best known at that time. All of them have been incredibly prolific, and their ideas are central to the growth of any number of fields.

148 One reviewer took me to task for not mentioning more queer writers who had dealt with sexuality, including Jewelle Gomez, Judy Grahn, Annie Sprinkle, Audre Lorde, Cheryle Clarke, Minnie Bruce Pratt, and Paula Allen Gunn. Interestingly, there were twelve women on the list some— many of which are mentioned in this section—but only three men.)

149 Hannah Witton, *Doing It: Let's Talk About Sex...* (London, England: Hachette UK, 2017).

150 Jack Halberstam, *Female Masculinity*. Durham, NC. Duke University Press, 2020. https://www.dukeupress.edu/female-masculinity-twentieth -anniversary-edition.

Chapter 2

1 "Read My Lips: Sexual Subversion and the End of Gender: Wilchins, Riki: 9781936833641: Amazon.com: Books," n.d., https://www.amazon.com/ Read-My-Lips-Sexual-Subversion/dp/1936833646.

2 *Critical Autoethnography: Intersecting Cultural Identities in Everyday Life* (Routledge & CRC Press, n.d.), https://www.routledge.com/Critical -Autoethnography-Intersecting-Cultural-Identities-in-Everyday-Life/ Boylorn-Orbe/p/book/9780367353032.

3 Some gay men refer to their anuses as their *cunts*.

4 Nor did I disconnect it from "boy," for that matter.

5 Talia Mae Bettcher, *Beyond Personhood: An Essay in Trans Philosophy* (Minneapolis: University of Minnesota Press, 2025).

6 "Beyond Personhood: An Essay in Trans Philosophy," Www.Jstor.Org, 2025, https://www.jstor.org/stable/10.5749/jj.17102153.

7 Hale, "Leatherdyke Boys and Their Daddies," 223.

8 Bettcher, "When Selves Have Sex."

9 Gayle S. Rubin, "Thinking Sex: Notes for a Radical Theory of the Politics of Sexuality," in *Culture, Society and Sexuality* (Routledge, 2007), 166–203, https://doi.org/10.4324/9780203966105-21.

10 Rubin, "Phenomenology as Method in Trans Studies."

11 Rubin explains, "Phenomenology joined with genealogy can historicize autobiographical accounts of identity without undermining the relevance of identity for the subjects inhabiting subject positions . . . [so that] discursive genealogy can historicize phenomenological accounts, while phenomenology can insert an embodied agent-in-progress into genealogical accounts."

12 Rubin, "Phenomenology as Method in Trans Studies."

13 Keegan, "Getting Disciplined: What's Trans About Queer Studies Now?," October 2018.

14 Talia Mae Bettcher, "Trans Women and Interpretive Intimacy: Some Initial Reflections," in *The Essential Handbook of Women's Sexuality*, ed. D. Castenada (Praeger, 2013), 51–68.

15 Of course, some readers will be reminded here of *Gender Trouble*'s famous analogy of sex versus gender, where the sex is to "the raw" as gender is to "the cooked." Her point was the sex was already gender, and so the distinction was apparent rather than real. In fact, she saw the understanding of sex as "raw," as a product of the gender system.

16 Stephanie L. Budge, Joe J. Orovecz, and Jayden L. Thai, "Trans Men's Positive Emotions: The Interaction of Gender Identity and Emotion Labels," *The Counseling Psychologist/the Counseling Psychologist* 43, no. 3 (February 13, 2015): 404–34, https://doi.org/10.1177/0011000014565715.

17 H. Howitt, "How We Fuck: Assembling Intimacy-as-Method to Research Trans Sex Practices," *Gender, Place & Culture* 31, no. 4 (2023): 523–42, https://doi.org/10.1080/0966369X.2023.2182738.

18 "Salmacian Home Page," n.d. https://salmacian.org/.

19 Sarah Emily Baum, "Trans People Are Seeking Nonbinary Bottom Surgeries," *Vice*, November 14, 2022, https://www.vice.com/en/article/4axp3n/trans-people-are-seeking-nonbinary-bottom-surgeries.

20 Cristan Williams, "Gender Performance: The TransAdvocate Interviews Judith Butler," TransAdvocate, n.d., https://www.transadvocate.com/gender-performance-the-transadvocate-interviews-judith-butler_n_13652.htm.

21 In a sense, she already has by uncharacteristically referring to the "self" twice.

22 For instance, see Slavo Žižek's "The Sexual Is Political" (Slavoj Žižek, "The Sexual Is Political—The Philosophical Salon," *The Philosophical Salon*, August 1, https://thephilosophicalsalon.com/the-sexual-is-political/).

23 This is not to say that there were no other nonbinary individuals since certainly there were, and there were also a number of cultural traditions which embrace individuals who may not identify as "nonbinary" but for whom we might consider the description fits.

24 Howitt, "How We Fuck."

25 Rubin, "Phenomenology as Method in Trans Studies," April 1, 1998.

26 Henry S. Rubin, "Reading Like a (Transsexual) Man," in *Men Doing Feminism*, Contributed Sandra Bartky, ed. Tom Digby (Taylor & Francis, December 19, 1997), https://www.taylorfrancis.com/books/edit/10.4324/9780203724231/men-feminism-sandra-bartky-tom-digby?refId=1a280963-b72d-4675-98b2-f267bfdf3b06&context=ubx.

27 Judith Butler, "Imitation and Gender Insubordination," *The Lesbian and Gay Studies Reader* (1993): n. 307–20.

28 This was written before Butler came out as nonbinary, so it is unclear if today she would still identify as a lesbian.

29 It would be inaccurate to refer to Butler's "lesbianism" now that they identify as nonbinary; however at that point, they were still identifying as such.

30 Butler, "Imitation and Gender Insubordination."

31 Julia Serano, *Whipping Girl: A Transsexual Woman on Sexism and the Scapegoating of Femininity*, 2nd ed. (Emeryville: Seal Press, 2007).

32 Bettcher, *Beyond Personhood.*

33 Rubin "Phenomenology as Method in Trans Studies."

34 Heather Love, "Queer Method and the Postwar History of Sexuality Studies (Part 1)," *Youtube*, July 15, 2014, https://www.youtube.com/watch?v =qkkZV6GkkKo.

35 Elfreda A. Chatman, "The Impoverished Life-World of Outsiders," *Journal of the American Society for Information Science*, Association for Information Science & Technology 47, no. 3 (March 1, 1996), https://doi .org/10.1002/(SICI)1097-4571(199603)47:3.

36 Chapman's studies highlighted the way impoverished people contribute to their own information poverty, by refusing to access knowledge sources outside their own small circle, distrusting outside sources of knowledge, and/or hiding their knowledge needs for fear of discrimination or stigma.

37 B. R. George and Stacey Goguen, "Hermeneutical Backlash," *Feminist Philosophy Quarterly* 7, no. 4 (December 6, 2021), https://doi.org/10.5206/ fpq/2021.4.13518.

38 Miranda Fricker, *Epistemic Injustice: Power and the Ethics of Knowing* (Oxford: Oxford University Press, 2007).

39 This of course results in many more young people coming out as trans than ever before, which is then used by the white, Christian nationalist right to ignite a moral panic—a *hermeneutical backlash* which refuses to recognize the new knowledge, instead endeavoring actively to refute, deny, and disconfirm it.

41 Moira Pérez, "Epistemic Violence: Reflections between the Invisible and the Ignorable," *El lugar sin límites* 1, no. 1 (2019): 81–98.

42 The metaphor is from *Gender Trouble* in which "'sex' is to nature or 'the raw' as gender is to culture or 'the cooked.'"

43 Chris Straayer, "Phantom Penis: Extrapolating Neuroscience and Employing Imagination for Trans Male Sexual Embodiment," *Studies in Gender and Sexuality* 21, no. 4 (October 1, 2020): 251–79, https://doi.org /10.1080/15240657.2020.1842075.

44 Rubin, "Reading Like a (Transsexual) Man."

45 A fact of which many survivors of incest are all too painfully aware— having been shocked and horrified by an involuntary physical reaction to acts that were vile and deeply disgusting.

46 Bettcher, "When Selves Have Sex."

47 Howitt, "How We Fuck."

48 Feministkilljoys, "Sweaty Concepts," Feministkilljoys, February 22, 2014, https://feministkilljoys.com/2014/02/22/sweaty-concepts.

49 Chu, "My New Vagina Won't Make Me Happy."

50 Michel Foucault, *Discipline and Punish: The Birth of the Prison* (New York: Penguin Group, 1977).

51 Laura Mulvey, "Visual Pleasure and Narrative Cinema," *Screen* 16, no. 3 (October 1, 1975): 6–18, https://doi.org/10.1093/screen/16.3.6.

52 "Suture: Trauma and Trans Becoming—Punctum Books," n.d., https:// punctumbooks.com/titles/suture-trauma-and-trans-becoming/. Santa Barbara.

53 Jules Gill-Peterson, "Dissociation as Trans Method; or, the Depressive's Technique," *Sad Brown Girl* (blog), May 7, 2021, https://sadbrowngirl .substack.com/p/dissociation-as-trans-method-or-the.

54 Tyler Fored, "My Life without Gender: 'Strangers Are Desperate to Know What Genitalia I Have,'" *The Guardian*, December 1, 2017, https://www .theguardian.com/world/2015/aug/07/my-life-without-gender-strangers -are-desperate-to-know-what-genitalia-i-have.

55 Susie Orbach, *Fat Is a Feminist Issue* (New York, 1978), https://openlibrary .org/books/OL1178918M/Fat_is_a_feminist_issue.

56 Personal communication with author, 2022.

57 I found this offhand comment both incredibly poignant but also very illuminating. Many of us have used mind-altering substances to deal with the pain of dysphoria, grief, or the hurts of transphobia.

58 Imogen Binnie, *Nevada* (New York: Topside Press, 2013).

59 María Lugones, "Gender and Universality in Colonial Methodology," *Critical Philosophy of Race* 8, no. 1–2 (January 1, 2020): 25–47, https://doi.org/10.5325/critphilrace.8.1-2.0025.

60 Plemons, "It Is as It Does: Genital Form and Function in Sex Reassignment Surgery."

61 Hil Malatino, "Future Fatigue: Trans Intimacies and Trans Presents (or How to Survive the Interregnum)," *Transgender Studies Quarterly* 6, no. 4 (November 1, 2019): 635–58, https://doi.org/10.1215/23289252-7771796.

62 "Healing the Broken Places: Transgender People Speak Out About Addiction & Recovery," Kindle Edition by Riki Wilchins.

63 Gershen Kaufman, *The Psychology of Shame: Theory and Treatment of Shame-based Syndromes* (New York: Springer Pub. Co., 1989).

64 "Gender Trouble: Feminism and the Subversion of Identity (New York: Routledge Classics) Butler, Judith: Books," n.d., https://www.amazon.com/Gender-Trouble-Feminism-Subversion-Routledge/dp/0415389550.

65 Chu, "My New Vagina Won't Make Me Happy."

66 Malatino, "Future Fatigue."

67 "Gender Trouble: Feminism and the Subversion of Identity (Routledge Classics): 9780415389556: Butler, Judith: Books."

68 P. Schilder, *The Image and Appearance of the Human Body* (Kegan Paul, 1935).

69 Henry S. Rubin, *Self-Made Men: Identity and Embodiment among Transsexual Men* (Nashville: Vanderbilt University Press, 2003), https://doi.org/10.2307/j.ctv17vf6c0.

70 J. O. Allen, V. Moïse, E. Solway, M. K. Cheney, D. J. Larson, P. N. Malani, D. Singer, and J. T. Kullgren, "How Old do I Look? Aging Appearance and Experiences of Aging among U.S. Adults Ages 50–80," *Psychology and Aging* 39, no. 5 (2024): 551–64, https://doi.org/10.1037/pag0000800.

71 The animosity toward so-called cankles might be considered an exception here, but I would argue it's more the product of trying to impose norms of femininity than of male appreciation for the erotic appeal of a feminine ankle.

72 Jill Burke, *How to Be a Renaissance Woman* (New York: Simon & Schuster, 2023), https://www.simonandschuster.com/books/How-to-Be-a-Renaissance-Woman/Jill-Burke/9781639365906.

73 Becca Rothfield, "A Delightful Look Back at How the Renaissance Changed Beauty Standards," *Washington Post*, December 14, 2023, https://www.washingtonpost.com/books/2023/12/14/how-be-renaissance-woman-jill-burke-review/.

74 https://en.wikipedia.org/wiki/Toplessness.

75 William Jankowiak, Justin R. Garcia, and Shelly Volsche, "The Half of the World That Doesn't Make Out," SAPIENS, February 10, 2016, https://www.sapiens.org/culture/is-romantic-kissing-a-human-universal/.

76 Wilchins, *Read My Lips*.

77 Admin, "Guest Post: Body Shaming Is Unacceptable, Even if Directed at Vile People. An Intersex Critique of 'Small Dick Energy,'" *Practical Ethics*, January 10, 2023, https://blog.practicalethics.ox.ac.uk/2023/01/guest-post-body-shaming-is-unacceptable-even-if-directed-at-vile-people-an-intersex-critique-of-small-dick-energy/.

78 "Anal Rejuvenation | Anal Reconstruction – Dr. Zuri Murrell," n.d., https://www.lacolonrectalsurgeon.com/additional-specialties/anal-rejuvenation/.

79 Gayle Salamon, *Assuming a Body: Transgender and Rhetorics of Materiality* (Columbia University Press, 2010), https://www.jstor.org/stable/10.7312/sala14958.

80 I have been dealing with Butler and Foucault for decades now, and it continues to surprise me how I still work my way around some particularly sticky epistemic corner to find some insight or other of theirs waiting for me.

81 Talia Mae Bettcher, "Evil Deceivers and Make-Believers: On Transphobic Violence and the Politics of Illusion," *Hypatia* 22, no. 3 (January 9, 2009): 43–65, https://doi.org/10.1111/j.1527-2001.2007.tb01090.x.

82 Quora, "As a Guy, Could I Apply for a Job as a Waiter at Hooters, Then Sue for Gender Discrimination When They Refuse to Hire Me? After All, I Ha...," n.d., https://www.quora.com/As-a-guy-could-I-apply-for-a-job-as-a-waiter-at-Hooters-then-sue-for-gender-discrimination-when-they-refuse-to-hire-me-After-all-I-have-experience-as-a-waiter-Im-great-with-customers-and-I-have-good-references. and Quora, "How Do Themed Restaurants Like Hooters or Twin Peaks Avoid Discrimination Lawsuits

When an Unattractive Girl or Man Applies for a Waitress...," n.d., https://www.quora.com/How-do-themed-restaurants-like-Hooters-or-Twin-Peaks-avoid-discrimination-lawsuits-when-an-unattractive-girl-or-man-applies-for-a-waitress-job.

84 Wataru Yamazaki and Yoshitsugu Tanino, "Gender Differences in Joint Torque Focused on Hip Internal and External Rotation During a Change in Direction While Walking," *Journal of Physical Therapy Science* 29, no. 12 (December 7, 2017): 2160–4, https://doi.org/10.1589/jpts.29.2160.

85 Reuters, "A Wiggle in the Walk Adds to Female Allure: Study," *Reuters*, August 9, 2007, https://www.reuters.com/article/us-wiggle/a-wiggle-in-the-walk-adds-to-female-allure-study-idUSN1626597220070316/.

86 Wilchins, *Read My Lips*.

87 Dickson D. Bruce Jr., "W. E. B. Du Bois and the Idea of Double Consciousness," *American Literature* 64, no. 2 (June 1, 1992): 299, https://doi.org/10.2307/2927837.

88 Rubin "Phenomenology as Method in Trans Studies."

89 Thomas Page McBee, "What I Saw in My First 10 Years on Testosterone," *New York Times*, June 25, 2021, https://www.nytimes.com/2021/06/25/opinion/transgender-transition-testosterone.html.

90 Plemons, "It Is as It Does: Genital Form and Function in Sex Reassignment Surgery."

91 Were you *really* expecting a footnote explaining this euphemism?

92 Bettcher, "Trans Women and Interpretive Intimacy," 51–68.

93 Malatino, "Future Fatigue."

94 Malatino, "Future Fatigue."

95 Or, at least it no longer feels dick-like.

96 Cotton, *Hung Jury: Testimonies of Genital Surgery by Transsexual Men*.

97 Howitt, "How We Fuck."

98 Malatino, "Future Fatigue."

99 Chu, "My New Vagina Won't Make Me Happy."

100 Shannon Sullivan and Nancy Tuana, *Race and Epistemologies of Ignorance* (Albany: State University of New York Press, 2007), https://doi.org/10.1353/book5200.

101 Talia Mae Bettcher, "What Is Trans Philosophy?," *Hypatia* 34, no. 4 (January 1, 2019): 644–67, https://doi.org/10.1111/hypa.12492.

102 With racism, that mean phenomena, such as white people in segregated Jim Crow towns who told themselves that Black residents also preferred it that way.

103 Bettcher, "What Is Trans Philosophy?."

104 Kristie Dotson, "Tracking Epistemic Violence, Tracking Practices of Silencing," *Hypatia* 26, No. 2 (2011): 236–57, https://www.jstor.org/stable/23016544.

105 David Bell, "Fucking Geography, Again," in *Geographies of Sexualities* (Routledge, 2017), 95–100.

106 Cáel M Keegan's "Getting Disciplined: What's Trans About Queer Studies Now?" is an outstanding example, although it was confined to academic. See: Cáel M. Keegan, "Getting Disciplined: What's Trans* About Queer Studies Now?" *Journal of Homosexuality* 67, no. 3 (2020): 384–97, https://doi.org/10.1080/00918369.2018.1530885. Epub 2018 October 22. PMID: 30346871.

107 Howitt, "How We Fuck,"

108 Bettcher, "What Is Trans Philosophy?."

109 Marilyn Frye, "In and out of Harm's Way," in *The Politics of Reality: Essays in Feminist Theory* (Trumansburg: Crossing Press, 1983), 52–84.

INDEX